LITTLE BOOK OF

VIKINGS

LITTLE BOOK OF

VIKINGS

First published in the UK in 2014

© Demand Media Limited 2014

www.demand-media.co.uk

Printed and bound in Europe

ISBN 978-1-910270-15-8

Contents

Introduction

From the fury of the Northmen, o Lord deliver us! The image of the Vikings as bloodthirsty, battle-hungry pirates, ruthless thugs and pillagers lingers to this day. If we are to believe the popular stereotype, the Viking, conveyed to his victims in a fearsome, dragon-prowed longboat and armed with a terrible axe, was intent on nothing more than plundering riches and spreading terror.

The truth about the Vikings is rather more complex. These Scandinavian peoples were also skilled seafarers who traded with the societies they met on their voyages and settled in the places they discovered. They ventured as far as Constantinople in the Middle East, the river Volga and even the Americas. They took with them a fascinating culture whose influence is felt to this day. They changed history.

While the British and Irish sometimes tend to think that their islands were the sole target of the men from what we know today as Norway, Sweden and Denmark, this is could not be further from the truth. The Viking influence was felt keenly in France and Spain. Vikings sailed through the Straits of Gibraltar, made their way through the Mediterranean and set foot in what is now known as Morocco. They settled in modern-day Russia, whose very name stems from that of a group of Vikings from Sweden. They troubled the mighty Byzantine Empire and knocked at the doors of Constantinople. They sailed north and west to colonise Iceland and Greenland and, when Leif Erikson settled in modern-day Canada, they became the first Europeans to set foot in North America, nearly 500 years before

Christopher Columbus.

The era known as the Viking Age is generally accepted as starting with a terrifying raid on Lindisfarne Abbey in 793 and ending with the events of 1066 that put a Norman king, himself the descendant of Vikings, on the English throne. There are few historical records of the time on which we can rely to piece the story of that era together; but luckily for us, there are some means.

Saga writers in the Viking colony of Iceland between the 12th and 14th centuries wrote down the stories of the heroes' exploits that had been handed down for centuries; we can decipher the runes the Scandinavians carved into thousands of stones where they lived; and archaeological investigations have provided us with deep insights into the Vikings' lives, culture, beliefs and deeds.

Some of the most important

archaeological finds have, since the middle of the 20th century, revealed extraordinary facets of Viking life. Burial sites tell us much about how Vikings lived, what they believed and what they considered important, for grave goods – articles buried with the deceased so they might use them in the afterlife – have been found in many places. Burial mounds in honour of mighty kings and chieftains – some of the most notable at Birka in Sweden, at the Borre mound cemetery in Norway and at Jelling in Denmark – have been found all over Scandinavia and beyond. Sometimes, as at Oseberg and Gokstad in Norway, entire ships were buried along with the bodies, giving archaeologists much to mull over.

These discoveries have done much to confirm what skilled shipbuilders and sailors the Vikings were. They built many types of vessel but the best known was the longship that so alarmed the victims of their raids – it was the longship that allowed them to 'go viking'. Capable of travelling at up to 15 knots, the longship was a long, narrow wooden boat with a shallow hull that allowed it to navigate in waters just a metre deep, and allowed beach landings. It was light, so that it could be carried, and double-ended so

its sailors could reverse direction quickly. Powered by oars as well as sail, longships were perfect for warfare.

And what warriors the Vikings could be. All free Norse men were allowed to carry weapons, but those high in the social scale would typically be equipped with helmet, shield, mail shirt and sword. Spears, short swords, shields and sometimes bows were used by lesser men, but the main battle weapon was the axe. The elite guardsmen, or housecarls, of the kings of England Cnut and Harold II, for example, wielded awe-inspiring two-handed axes that could split the shields or helmets of their enemies with ease. One thing the Vikings never had, contrary to popular belief, was the horned helmet.

When they went into battle with their customary violence – and we know that their reputation for aggression was second to none – the Vikings would be taking inspiration from their belief and trust in their gods. The Norse religion offered such deities as the hammer-wielding Thor, god of thunder and lightning, war and the protection of mankind, and Odin, the Allfather of the gods also associated with war as well as with victory and death.

To engage in combat with Vikings was to meet men fighting in furious, frenetic

style. Their shock troops – sometimes called Odin's special warriors – were the berserkers, who fought in a nigh-uncontrollable, trance-like fury that has given us the word berserk. It's commonly thought nowadays that berserkers could work themselves into this rage, but there is a school of thought that believes they may have been fighting under the influence of hallucinogenic mushrooms or huge amounts of alcohol. One source tells us these men 'went without their mailcoats and were mad as hounds or wolves, bit their shields … they slew men, but neither fire nor iron had effect upon them.'

Then there were the Vikings in times of peace, people who settled, farmed and traded just as they had back home in Scandinavia. We will look at how these people lived and worked, how their complex societies were structured and at their beliefs and their culture. We can accompany them on their voyages as they widened their spheres of influence throughout the known world and beyond, and we will see how the sagas related their deeds of exploration and derring-do. We will see how their fame and impact live on today. Welcome to the world of the Vikings.

Who Were the Vikings?

They helped to shape the world as we know it today. Some of history's most momentous events – including the European discovery of North America and William's conquest of England in 1066 – stemmed from their explorations, interventions and conquests. Their character, culture and beliefs still have the power to fascinate. So who were these extraordinary people; who were the Vikings?

The simple answer is that they were farming and fishing folk from the lands that make up modern Scandinavia – Norway, Sweden and Denmark – and eventually Iceland. Not all people from these regions were Vikings, however, for the word came to mean pirates, raiders from the sea who travelled vast distances to plunder and pillage. To get an idea of how this association came about, it's necessary to examine the word 'Viking'.

The term first surfaced in Old English; in the Anglo-Saxon Chronicle it is used three times to refer to robbers who preyed on coastal communities. Some experts believe that this usage mirrored the development of a word in Old Norse that came from the same ancient Germanic root – a verb meaning to leave or depart. Others think that 'viking' is related to an Old Icelandic word for a bay or creek. And there are other theories: it comes from an Old Icelandic word meaning 'turn aside'; from an Old English noun, 'wic', meaning an armed camp; from the old word 'vika', which meant a turn on duty for an oarsman; or even from the name of those who left the area of Vik around Oslofjord for raids on England.

Whatever the true origin of the word, we know that 'wicing' was being used

Above:
*Leif Erikson
discovers North
America. Photo
Nasjonalgalleriet
Oslo*

by the 10th century to refer to sea raiders from the Scandinavian region. But this was a very different part of the world to the one we know today.

Countries such as Denmark and Sweden didn't exist. The first Scandinavians who ventured out on 'a viking' were men whose loyalty lay with the leaders of particular regions such as Jutland, Hordaland and Vestfold. They spoke a common language, however –

the one we know now as Old Norse – and had certain aspects of their daily lives in common – their dress, their religion, their customs and their art. The first Vikings were, for most of the year, fishermen and farmers living in subsistence economies who, in the summer, would follow the call of their local leaders for crews to venture across the sea and seek opportunities for raiding, trading or finding new lands to settle. They were, in effect, part-time

Above: *Viking farmers' cart. Photo Museum of Cultural History, University of Oslo, Norway. Photographer Eirik Irgens Johnsen*

warriors and explorers.

As time went on, national identities began to form, and the peoples of southern Scandinavia came to be known as Danes while their cousins in the north were referred to as Norse. And as time went on, the word 'Viking' took on new meanings.

By the 13th century it was being used in Icelandic sagas to mean 'pirates' but its use was scarce in western Europe during the Middle Ages. It was not until the 19th century, a period of history marked by the rise of nationalist movements in

Europe, that it came to be used again in Scandinavia. Its first mention in modern English came as late as 1807/08, and Sir Walter Scott seized upon it for use in his 1822 novel The Pirate.

By now the romantic idea of the Viking as a noble savage was taking hold in the public imagination, leading to renewed interest and the so-called 19th century Viking Revival. The effect of the upsurge in interest in the Vikings – and the plundering of their history for the purposes of popular entertainment – has led to the over-simplified modern view of these people as violent, pagan barbarians and courageous explorers. Vikings could be both of these things, but the popular image does not come anywhere near explaining the whole truth.

Likewise, it's a little too simple to define the start of the Viking Age as 793AD, when raiders destroyed the abbey on the Holy Island of Lindisfarne, and the end as the Norman Conquest of England in 1066. There is evidence of earlier contact between people from Scandinavia and other lands, in the form of English and Irish artefacts in graves in Norway dating from the eighth century. Perhaps these artefacts were stolen, or maybe they had been traded; we cannot say. What they do indicate is that there had been some kind of contact between peoples of various lands before 793.

We also know that people from what is now Sweden had been intent on expanding in the Baltic before 793. And we know that some of the characteristics associated with the Viking Age – such as the establishment of towns, contact and trading with overseas communities, increased production and a movement from exchange to market-based trade – had begun to emerge in southern Scandinavia well before the events of

Lindisfarne. The formation of states and expansion from the Scandinavian base began well before the date set out in the history books as the start of the Viking Age.

We will examine what drove the people who came to be known as Vikings to venture beyond their Scandinavian homes in the next chapter, but in order to understand their motives for foreign adventure, it's necessary to know a little about their ways of life – which nonetheless varied widely between different areas, for the climate and geography of southern Denmark is very different to that in the far north of Norway.

Nevertheless, as in all subsistence economies, the principle occupation of Scandinavians was the production of food, and this took the form of farming, fishing, trapping and the gathering in of crops and natural products. Communities were obliged to be largely self-sufficient, and they were also required to possess skills in the making of tools and equipment from whatever raw materials their local areas provided. These skills of self-sufficiency and ingenuity were to serve the men from the north well as they ventured away from their homes in search of new opportunities.

Motives for Expansion

The victims of Viking pirate raids may not have cared why their persecutors had decided to descend on their settlements – the very fact that they were there, pillaging, plundering and murdering, was more than enough to contemplate. But if we are to understand the Vikings, it's important to answer the question 'why?' At a time when overseas travel was hazardous and rare, and many people never set foot outside the settlement in which they were born, what spurred the Scandinavians on to venture out from the homelands?

The problem in answering this all-important question is that there is a great deal of debate about the Vikings' motivations for expansion. It's something historians continue to argue, with discussion often focusing on whether there was a single reason and if and how the motives changed over time. Perhaps we can simplify the argument by stating that overseas quests began against a background of growth in Scandinavian populations and a resultant competition for resources, and evolved into searches for wealth and new land to colonise. We thus come up against the age-old question: were the Vikings primarily raiders, or was their emphasis on trading and settlement?

But we have no real evidence to show that overseas expansion was absolutely vital to accommodate population growth in Scandinavia – there seems to have been ample suitable land available at home to cater for a burgeoning number of mouths to feed. Is it more probable that expansion was driven by the threat posed to local chieftains by regional rivals who were looking to extend their territories,

or unite neighbouring regions into more powerful kingdoms?

There is conflicting evidence as to whether Vikings travelled overseas specifically in order to settle new lands, too. Some parts of the lands to which they ventured, such as England and Ireland, seem to have been subjected to many decades of plundering before the Vikings made any attempt to settle. On the other hand, the islands to the west and north of Scotland and areas around the Baltic Sea seem to have been settled relatively soon after the Vikings first made contact with their communities. And the method of settlement varied, too. Sometimes land was taken by force; sometimes it was passed on to the new owners after an agreement had been reached with the previous ones.

We may do better, in looking for a reason for early Viking expansion, to focus on the importance of portable wealth to local leaders. As centres of power gradually coalesced in Scandinavia, chieftains took part in an economy based on the exchange of gifts, with their status based on portable wealth that could be passed down the hierarchy as rewards for loyalty to people of lower rank. We know from the sagas that powerful leaders were known to give silver arm rings to their followers, and hoards of silver have often been found in Scandinavia and in locations of Viking raids.

In turn, the leaders, who often had access to imported goods denied to lesser mortals, accepted tribute from those in a weaker position. And if no gifts were forthcoming, well, the option of using force to obtain them was open to a chieftain.

The acquisition of wealth by force is exemplified by archaeological finds of hoards of extraordinary value, like the one found on the banks of the river Ribble at Cuerdale in Lancashire. Left, but never retrieved, by Vikings who had been expelled from Dublin around 900AD, the hoard contained around 7,500 coins and 1,000 pieces of silver in ingots and ornaments such as silver arm rings. Modern estimates put its value at between £300,000 and £4 million.

It was probably the result of both raiding and trading, for the Scandinavians were taking a lead in the development of trade between areas in which they were active – even acting as middlemen between east and west. When the Mediterranean Sea became closed to international trade, Vikings sought out new routes via the Baltic and Russia, and they opened up new relationships with merchants from other lands wherever they went.

Later, as the importance of the exchange of gifts declined, the status provided by the possession of land rose to prominence. And so Viking expeditions came to focus on the acquisition of places for settlement, whether they were in the north Atlantic – where there were few people to object – or in places like the British Isles, where territories had to be taken by force. Viking leaders were now able to acquire land from abbeys and kings and redistribute it to their followers, although there is even some evidence that land in England was purchased for hard cash. The Vikings' silver, once used in the practice of gift giving, had been given a very different purpose.

So it's probable that the Vikings' motives for exploration, raiding, trading and expansion of territory changed over time. What we can be certain of is that the Scandinavians' gift for development of ocean-going means of transport served them well. And we can tell from archaeological evidence that the various reasons for expansion brought about very different types of vessel. Different ship types served different purposes.

In 1957 the Danish National Museum salvaged five ships from the Roskilde fjord – they had been scuttled there around 1070, it seems, in order to block the fjord entrance and protect a royal centre. It emerged, naturally, that the shipbuilders of the 11th century were adept at producing the famous longships, slender in form, designed for rapidity over the waves, driven by oars and sail and perfect for waging sea-borne war. But they also built more solid, wider vessels, relying purely on sails for propulsion except when

becalmed or when manoeuvring, for the purpose of transporting cargo, and smaller vessels that were used for fishing and for ferrying passengers short distances.

Not all of the Vikings' ships were the dreaded, speedy longships with striped sails and a dragon at their prows that persist in the popular imagination. Despite what you see in the movies, the Vikings were about more than rape and pillage.

Above: *Viking saddle mount. Photo Borre Museum of Cultural History, University of Oslo, Norway. Photographer Eirik Irgens Johnsen*

Vikings in the British Isles

It was more or less inevitable that the first Viking assault on the British Isles, when it took place in the last decade of the eighth century, would fall on a Christian monastery. Communities of monks had been set up on small isles and in coastal sites all around the islands, so that the holy men could live in seclusion and peace and devote themselves to their duties and prayer without fear of interference. The decision to base themselves far from large settlements was to backfire for, unprotected and isolated, they proved easy prey for the raiders.

Historians have remarked that the first Vikings to set foot in the British Isles would have been amazed to find so many communities of great wealth whose inhabitants were entirely unarmed. It's easy to see that, far from being specifically anti-Christian in nature – and it should

be borne in mind that the raids on the monasteries would have given many of the aggressors their first contact with Christians – the attacks were simply chosen for the ease with which they could be accomplished.

For all the alarm the attack on Lindisfarne caused, it was not the first time Vikings had come ashore in these islands; the first raid on Anglo-Saxon England that we know of came four years before those fateful events. In 789, three ships from Hordaland, nowadays a county in Norway, made landfall in the Isle of Portland, then part of the kingdom of Wessex. The duty of the reeve of Dorchester – a man elected every year to supervise lands for a lord – was to identify every foreign merchant who entered the kingdom, and this he did in the case of the visiting Scandinavians. Unfortunately for the reeve, his mistake

in identifying the raiders as merchants did not go unpunished, and when he urged them to accompany him to the king's manor to pay a trading tax, they murdered him instead.

We do not know for certain, but we can be fairly confident that further exploratory Viking raids took place soon after the Portland incident and before the attack on Lindisfarne. In 792, King Offa of Mercia – he who was responsible for the raising of Offa's Dyke between his kingdom and Wales – started to arrange for Kent to be defended against raids by men described as pagan peoples.

And then, in 793, came the sacking of Lindisfarne Priory on Holy Island off the coast of Northumbria, and the beginning of what is commonly called the Viking Age. The Anglo-Saxon Chronicle recorded: 'In this year fierce, foreboding omens came over the land of the Northumbrians, and the wretched people shook; there were excessive whirlwinds, lightning and fiery dragons were seen flying in the sky. These signs were followed by great famine, and a little after those, that same year on sixth ides of January, the ravaging of wretched heathen people destroyed God's church at Lindisfarne.' In fact the generally accepted date of the attack on Lindisfarne is June 8, but historical accuracy was never the Anglo-Saxons' strong point.

A more detailed and accurate description of the assault was recorded in History of the Church of Durham by the monk Simeon. He wrote: 'On the seventh of the ides of June, they reached the church of Lindisfarne, and there they miserably ravaged and pillaged everything; they trod the holy things under their polluted feet, they dug down the altars, and plundered all the treasures of the church. Some of the brethren they slew, some they carried off with them in chains, the greater number they stripped naked, insulted, and cast out of doors, and some they drowned in the sea.'

The events of Lindisfarne caused tremors throughout these islands, and it was not to be long before Vikings revisited Northumbria's shores: in 794 they sacked the nearby Monkwearmouth-Jarrow Abbey, an institution that had produced the great Anglo-Saxon scholar Bede. Then, in 1795, they turned their attentions to a Scottish island, raiding Iona Abbey on the west coast. This particular monastery was to be attacked twice more, in 802 and 806, when no fewer than 68 inhabitants were killed. This was quite enough for the Iona monks who, fearing further raids, fled to Kells in Ireland.

As the ninth century dawned, Vikings began to attack coastal districts in Ireland, and a little later, in 835, the first major raid in southern England took place when the Isle of Sheppey, off the coast of Kent, was raided. Sheppey was later to play host to an occupying force, when Vikings spent the winter of 855 there.

Unsurprisingly given the Vikings' apparent lust for portable wealth, hoards of treasure were being buried in England around this time. Some were doubtless interred by Anglo-Saxons trying to hide their riches from the raiders, but perhaps others were buried by the Vikings themselves to protect their loot, to which they would return at a later date.

A hoard discovered in Croydon, to the south of London, in 1862 contained 250 coins, three complete silver ingots and part of a fourth as well as four fragments of silver in a linen bag – rich pickings for the Viking army in question. Archaeologists believe this hoard had been buried in 872 as the army was spending the winter in London. And the scope of the Vikings' expeditions can be gauged from the fact that the coins had been gathered from a vast geographical area: there was coinage from Wessex, Mercia and East Anglia as well as imports from the Carolingian dynasty of Francia and even the Arab world. Not all Viking hoards in England contained coins; 19 silver ingots were discovered at Bowes Moor in Durham, for example, while a silver neck ring and a brooch were found at Orton Scar in Cumbria.

By the time the ninth century was halfway through, the people of Britain's lack of preparation to repel Viking raids had made larger-scale operations pretty much inevitable. The Scandinavians began to see the islands as locations for potential colonisation rather than simply raiding, and larger armies began to arrive, intent on conquering land and building settlements.

In 866, Viking armies captured York, one of the two major cities in Anglo-Saxon England. Five years later, King Ethelred of Wessex, who had been the leader of the struggle against the Vikings, died, and his place on the throne was taken by his younger brother, Alfred the Great. Many Anglo-Saxon kings had meanwhile begun to capitulate to the Vikings' demands and hand over land for settlements to them. The Northumbrian monarch Helafdene gave up his lands in 876 and over the next four years the invaders gained further land in the kingdoms of Mercia and East Anglia.

Alfred, meanwhile, had been continuing the conflict with the invading forces that had been begun by his brother, but he was driven back into the Somerset Levels, in the south-west of his kingdom, in 878, taking refuge in a fort in the marshes of Athelney. It was from here that the popular legend grew of Alfred being given shelter by a peasant woman who, unaware of his identity, left him to watch some cakes she had left cooking on the fire. Preoccupied with the problems posed by the Viking invaders, Alfred accidentally let the cakes burn, or so the legend goes.

But his fortunes were about to improve. Alfred regrouped his forces and, in May 878, defeated the armies of the Viking ruler of East Anglia, Guthrum, at the Battle of Edington. The defeated Danes retreated to Chippenham, where Alfred laid siege and forced their surrender, insisting as he did so that Guthrum be baptised a Christian, with Alfred acting as his godfather. The peace lasted until 844, when Guthrum attacked again, only to be defeated once more. Following this reverse, Guthrum joined Alfred in signing the Treaty of Wedmore in 886.

The result of the treaty was the establishment of a boundary between the Norse-controlled kingdom of East Anglia and Alfred's Wessex. The area to the north and east of the boundary became known as the Danelaw because it was under the control of the Norsemen, while those areas to the south and west of it remained under Anglo-Saxon rule. The Danelaw consisted, roughly, of 15 shires: Yorkshire; the Five Boroughs of Leicester, Nottingham, Derby, Stamford and Lincoln; Essex; the East Anglian shires of Cambridgeshire, Suffolk and Norfolk; and the East Midlands shires of Northamptonshire, Huntingdonshire and Bedfordshire.

Alfred capitalised on the agreement by setting about the construction of a series of defended towns, began to build a navy and organised a militia system under which half of his peasant army was on active service. His measures were successful: although there were continuous attacks on Wessex by new Viking armies, the kingdom's new defences held, and in 896 the invaders dispersed to settle in East Anglia and Northumbria, while others sailed off to Normandy.

Alfred's policy of opposing the Viking settlers was continued under the regime of his eldest daughter Ethelflaed, whom he had married to Ethelred, Lord of the Mercians, and under her son, Edward the Elder. In 920 the Northumbrian and Scots governments both submitted to the military power of Wessex, and in 937 the Battle of Brunanburh led to the collapse of Norse power in northern Britain. In 954 Erik Bloodaxe, the last Norse King of York, was expelled from the city and driven out of Northumbria.

If the English thought that was the last they would see of Viking invaders, they could not have been more wrong. England was further unified under the reign of the Wessex king Edgar the Peaceful, with Edgar coming to be recognised as the ruler of all England by both the Anglo-Saxon and Norse populations. But the strength of the English monarchy was about to

wane under the regimes of Edgar's son Edward the Martyr, who was murdered in 978, and then Ethelred the Unready. Scandinavian eyes were turning once again towards England, and in 980 Viking raiders launched a new wave of attacks.

England's rulers decided that the best way of dealing with these attackers was to pay them protection money – it was to become known Danegeld from the 12th century onwards – and in 991 they gave them £10,000. As is the case with many protection rackets, this enormous sum did not satisfy the Vikings, and over the next decade the English kingdom was forced to hand over increasingly large amounts of money. Many English began to demand that a more hostile approach be taken against the Vikings, recalling the approach of Alfred the Great, and Ethelred was told that the Scandinavians in England 'would faithlessly take his life, and then all his councillors, and possess his kingdom afterwards', according to the Anglo-Saxon Chronicle. In response, Ethelred 'ordered slain all the Danish men who were in England'.

In what came to be known as the Saint Brice's Day Massacre, on 13 November 1002 mass killings took place – historians believe there was a very large loss of life. Among those thought to have been slaughtered were Gunhilde, who was possibly the sister of King Sweyn I of Denmark – otherwise known as Sweyn Forkbeard – and her husband Pallig Tokesen, the Danish lord of Devonshire.

It was in revenge for this example of ethnic cleansing, and perhaps in particular for the killing of his sister, that Forkbeard launched raids on England between 1002 and 1005, and again between 1006 and 1007 and 1009 and 1012. Another version of history is uncertain about Sweyn's involvement in these excursions but favours the possibility that he exploited the confusion caused by raids by Thorkell the Tall, who was a Jomsviking – thought to be a band of mercenaries and brigands.

In 1013 Sweyn was definitely at the forefront as he launched a full-scale invasion of England. The Peterborough Chronicle tells us: 'Before the month of August came King Sweyn with his fleet to Sandwich. He went very quickly about East Anglia into the Humber's mouth, and so upward along the Trent till he came to Gainsborough. Earl Uchtred and all Northumbria quickly bowed to him, as did all the people of Lindsey, then the people of the Five Boroughs. He was given hostages from each shire.

'When he understood that all the people had submitted to him, he bade that his force should be provisioned and horsed; he went south with the main part of the invasion force, while some of the invasion force, as well as the hostages, were with his son Cnut. After he came over Watling Street, they went to Oxford, and the town-dwellers soon bowed to him, and gave hostages. From there they went to Winchester and the people did the same, then eastward to London.'

It seems that the people of London – among whom were Ethelred and Thorkell the Tall, who had defected to the former's side – put up a stern resistance against the rampaging Scandinavians. Sweyn swung west to Bath, where the thanes submitted and presented him with hostages. Soon enough the Londoners, in fear of what Sweyn might do if they resisted any longer, did likewise.

Ethelred was in retreat, first sending his sons Edward and Alfred to Normandy and then following them into exile after a period spent on the Isle of Wight. It had taken Sweyn just a few short months to submit England to his will, and he was declared king on Christmas Day 1013.

His reign did not last long – a mere five weeks, in fact. Having based himself in Gainsborough and started to organise affairs, Sweyn died in February 1014. At first he was succeeded as king of Denmark by his elder son, Harald II, but the Danish fleet proclaimed his younger son Cnut king. In England, the councillors sent for Ethelred, who on his return from exile in the spring of 1014 managed to drive Cnut out of England.

Once again, peace did not reign for long. Cnut returned with another army in 1016, and after vanquishing the Anglo-Saxon forces at the Battle of Assandun – near either Saffron Walden or Rochford, but by all accounts somewhere in Essex – Cnut became king of England, ruling over both the Danish and English kingdoms. Following Cnut's death in 1035, the two kingdoms were once more declared independent and remained apart until 1040 when Cnut's son, Harthacnut, took possession of the English throne.

He was the last Danish king to rule England. His sudden death in 1042 – reportedly following a drinking bout at a wedding – brought Magnus I to the throne in Denmark and the Anglo-Saxon Edward the Confessor to power in England, despite the claims to the throne of Magnus and his heir, Harald Hardrada. Edward's death in 1066 brought matters to a head.

His successor, Harold Godwinson, was challenged by Hardrada, by now king of Denmark. The ensuing Battle of Stamford Bridge, in the East Riding of Yorkshire, took place on 25 September 1066, and pitted the English army under Harold against the invading Norwegian forces of Hardrada and none other than the English king's brother, Tostig Godwinson. The pair had already defeated a hastily gathered army of English at Fulford. Stamford Bridge was a blood-soaked battle, and at the end of it both Hardrada and Tostig lay dead, along with most of their fellow invaders.

Harold's rejoicing – if any; he had overseen the death of his brother, after all – was short-lived. He had a battered, depleted and exhausted army which, having been forced to hasten north to combat the invasion, was now being asked to speed to the south coast, where it would encounter the army of another claimant to the throne – Duke William II of Normandy, himself a descendant of Vikings.

Few readers will need reminding of the events of the Battle of Hastings of October 1066, when Harold Godwinson was killed and his army defeated by William, who was henceforth the Conqueror and king. He was crowned king of England on December 25 of that year, although it was several years before he was able to bring the kingdom under his complete control.

The battles of Stamford Bridge and Hastings are often held up as representing the end of the Viking era in England, but they were not the final instances of Scandinavian involvement in English affairs. Just four years after Hastings, the Danish king Sweyn Estridsson sailed up the Humber with an army in support of Edgar the Aetheling, the last male member of the royal House of Wessex. Edgar had been proclaimed king in 1066, but never crowned. After capturing York, Sweyn took a payment from William on condition that he deserted Edgar's cause.

Five years later, one of Sweyn's sons sailed for England to support another English rebellion, but it had been crushed before they arrived, so they settled for plundering York and the surrounding area before returning home. In 1085 Canute IV of Denmark, with designs on the English throne, assembled a major invasion fleet, but it never sailed. After that, there were no serious invasions or raids of England by Scandinavians. What had started with a few Vikings being mistaken for merchants in Wessex nearly

300 hundred years before was at an end.

Meanwhile, events in Scotland, following the first Viking raid on the monastery of Iona in 794, had followed a different path. It's believed that Scandinavian presence in Scotland increased in the 830s and in 839 a Norse fleet invaded via the rivers Tay and Earn and reached into the heart of the Pictish kingdom of Fortriu. The Vikings defeated the king of the Picts, Eogán mac Óengusa, his brother Bran and the king of the Scots of Dál Riata, Áed mac Boanta, besides many Pictish aristocrats. The kingdom they had built and the Pictish leadership fell apart.

By the middle of the ninth century, Scandinavians had settled in Shetland, Orkney, the Hebrides and the Isle of Man, and some parts of mainland Scotland, to some extent integrating with the local Gaelic population in the Hebrides and Man. These areas were ruled over by local jarls, originally captains of ships. The jarl of Orkney and Shetland, however, claimed supremacy.

In 875, King Harald Fairhair led a fleet from Norway to Scotland, having found in his attempt to unite his country that many of those opposed to him had sought refuge in the Isles, from where they were

LITTLE BOOK OF **VIKINGS**

raiding foreign lands including Norway itself. He organised a fleet and was able to subdue the rebels, and in doing so brought the independent jarls under his control, many of the rebels having fled to Iceland. Fairhair thus found himself ruling not only Norway but also the Isles, Man and parts of mainland Scotland.

In 876 a fleet led by Ketil Bjornsson, known as Flatnose, was sent to regain control of Man and the Hebrides after those peoples had rebelled against Harald's rule. Following his success, Ketil was to rule the southern isles – or Sudreys – as a vassal of Harald. His grandson, Thorstein the Red, and Sigurd the Mighty, jarl of Orkney, invaded Scotland and were able to exact tribute from nearly half the kingdom until they fell in battle. Ketil declared himself King of the Isles but was eventually outlawed and fled to Iceland.

The Kings of the Isles continued to act semi-independently, in 973 forming a defensive pact with the kingdoms of Scotland and Strathclyde. In 1095, the King of Man and the Isles, Godred Crovan, was killed by the Norwegian king, Magnus Barelegs, whereupon Magnus and King Edgar of Scotland agreed a treaty: the islands would be ruled by Norway while the mainland territories would go to Scotland. Thus the king of Norway continued to be the nominal king of the Isles and Man.

But in 1156 the kingdom was split in two. The Western Isles and Man continued to be known as the Kingdom of Man and the Isles, but the Inner Hebrides came under the influence of Somerled, a Gaelic speaker who was styled King of the Hebrides. Somerled's kingdom was later to develop into the Lordship of the Isles.

The true end of the Viking age in Scotland is considered to have come in 1266. In 1263, Haakon IV of Norway arrived on the west coast with a fleet from Norway and Orkney, seeking revenge for a Scots expedition to Skye, and joined the fleets of King Magnus of Man and King Dougal of the Hebrides. Negotiations proved fruitless, and his forces met the Scots in battle at Largs in Ayrshire. The battle proved indecisive in all but one aspect: it ensured that the Norse were not able to follow up with a further attack that year. Haakon died while spending the winter in Orkney, and by 1266 his son, Magnus the Law-Mender, had ceded the Kingdom of Man and the Isles, with all territories on mainland Scotland, to Alexander III through the Treaty of Perth.

Wales did not meet a similar outcome

Opposite: *King Alfred in the Danish Camp, by Joseph Martin Kronheim*

to Viking incursions as its neighbours to the east and north. It was not colonised significantly, but the Vikings did settle in small numbers in the south around St Davids, Haverfordwest and the Gower Peninsula, and place names such as Skokholm, Skomer and Swansea are reminders of the Norse presence. The Welsh kings were powerful, however, and Scandinavians were never able to exert the same kind of influence over their kingdom as they did in England and Scotland.

But following a Viking alliance with Brittany in 865 the Britons made peace with the Danes, and a Viking/Welsh alliance defeated an Anglo-Saxon army from Mercia in 878. Although the Welsh had long been enemies of Mercia, relations with Wessex were rather warmer, and the Anglo-Saxon Chronicle refers to Vikings being pursued by a force of West Saxons and north Welsh along the River Severn in 893.

The city of Swansea was founded by Sweyn Forkbeard – the name comes from the Old Norse for Sweyn's Island. The neighbouring Gower has some place names of Norse origin, too: Worm's Head comes from the Norse word for dragon, for the Vikings believed the island, shaped like a snake, was a sleeping dragon.

Across the Irish Sea, there was a very different story of Viking invasion and settlement. The Scandinavians launched numerous raids on Ireland and founded many towns, including Dublin, Limerick, Wexford, Waterford and Leixlip.

The first raiders, who had journeyed from Norway, appeared in Irish waters at the end of the eighth century, just as they did in England. The first recorded attack took place in 795 on Rathlin Island off the coast of Antrim, where the church was burned. The west-coast monasteries on Inismurray and Inisbofin were also plundered; it's possible the same raiders were responsible, and it should not be overlooked that the Scottish island of Iona was attacked in the same year.

Until around 836 the raids followed a clear hit-and-run pattern, and they were carried out by small, probably independent freebooters on coastal targets – no Viking raid is recorded for areas further inland than 20 miles. The attacks were difficult to defend but the Vikings didn't always have it all their way. In 811 a raiding party was slaughtered by the people of Ulster and the following year attacks were beaten off by the men of Umaill in the west. By 823 the Vikings had covered the

entire coast with their raids, and in 824 the island monastery of Sceilg, off the coast of Kerry, was attacked. The monastic city of Armagh came in for assault no fewer than three times in 832.

In the first quarter century of Viking attacks there was an average of one raid a year, which can have caused no great distress in Irish society; attacks on monasteries were common before the Viking Age and the burning of churches was an integral part of Irish warfare. Moreover, wars had broken out between monasteries before the coming of the Vikings. But from around 830, the raids became more intense.

In 832, for instance, there were extensive plunderings in the lands of the Cianachta near the sea in Louth. In 836 raiders attacked the land of the O'Neills of southern Brega and launched raids in Connacht. In 837, two fleets of 60 ships each appeared on the Boyne and the Liffey, and soon afterwards Vikings made their way up the Shannon and the Erne and put a fleet on Lough Neagh.

The Vikings established longphorts (ship enclosures or shore fortresses) at Annagassan in Louth and at Dublin in 1841, using them as bases for attacks in the south and west. They wintered for the first time at Dublin in 841-842 and in 842 another large fleet arrived.

The first reference to co-operation between Vikings and Irish dates to that year, although it may have happened before. A fleet based on Lough Ree and the Shannon built a fortified position on the shores of Lough Ree, from where Scandinavians ravaged the countryside in 844. Mael Seachnaill, overking of the O'Neills, retaliated, attacking the Vikings, capturing a leader called Turgesius and drowning him in Lough Owel in Westmeath. From now on, Irish kings followed his example and started to fight back.

Because they now had fixed settlements, the Vikings were more vulnerable to attack. Seachnaill routed a Scandinavian army near Skreen, County Meath, killing 700 of them, and at Castledermot in Kildare the united armies of Munster and Leinster defeated a large force of Vikings. The newly founded Viking settlement at Cork was destroyed and in 849 Seachnaill ravaged the Norse territory of Dublin. The Vikings were by now accepted as a factor in the internal politics of Ireland and alliances between Norse and Irish became commonplace.

Between 849 and 852 a new phenomenon arose: Vikings fighting between themselves. New Vikings, probably from Denmark, arrived in the Irish Sea and battles took place between the new arrivals and the more established Scandinavians. In 853 Olaf the White arrived in Dublin and with Ivar, another Viking, assumed sovereignty of the Viking settlement there.

Vikings at Waterford attacked the King of Osraige but were slaughtered in 860; a longphort settlement at Youghal was destroyed in 866; in 887 the Limerick Vikings were killed by the men of Connacht; and in 892 the Vikings of Waterford, Wexford and St Mullins were defeated. Ivar, joint king of Dublin, died in 873 and struggles and division filled the city for next two decades. In 902 the kings of Brega and Leinster defeated the Norse of Dublin, destroyed their settlement and expelled them from Ireland.

By this time, Irish and Norse cultures had become extensively assimilated. Olaf, king of Dublin in the middle of the ninth century, was married to the daughter of Aed Findliath (the Fair Warrior), king of the northern O'Neills, and the Hiberno-Norse had gradually become Christianised. The annals, recording the death of Ivar in 872, said 'he rested in

Christ'.

By the first decades of the 10th century opportunities for Vikings in Britain and mainland Europe were limited, so it's not surprising that they chose to attack Ireland again. From 914 large fleets, manned by Vikings from Britain, launched assaults. Munster was ravaged in 915, the king of Tara was defeated when he went to the aid of the Munstermen and the king of Leinster was killed in a battle with Vikings at Leixlip. The king of Tara was killed in a combined Irish attack on the Norse of Dublin in 919.

During the next two decades the Norse kings of Dublin were trying to establish their power in York, so their Irish activities became confined to Dublin and its immediate hinterland. The Irish began to counter-attack with growing success: Dublin was burned by the king of Tara in 936 and was sacked in 944. By the second half of the 10th century its power was considerably reduced.

One of the great leaders of this period was Brian Boru of County Clare, who had defeated the Vikings of Munster and whose great rival was Mael Seachnaill II, King of Tara who had defeated the Norse of Dublin in 980. Brian sometimes made alliances with the Scandinavians, as in 984

when the Norse of Waterford attacked Leinster by sea while he attacked by land. In 977, Brian and Mael Seachnaill sealed an agreement whereby the former would be king of the southern part of Ireland while the latter would rule the north. In 998 the two kings co-operated in an attack on Dublin.

The following year the Dublin Norse, allied with Leinster, revolted but were defeated by Brian. He spent January and February 1000 plundering Dublin, destroying its fortress and expelling the king Sitric, who upon giving hostages to Brian was restored. Brian now claimed the kingship of the whole island and Mael Seachnaill submitted.

In 1012, Leinster, with the aid of the Dublin Norse, revolted against Brian. He and Mael Seachnaill attacked Leinster and blockaded Dublin from September to Christmas before returning home. Knowing the attack would be renewed, the Norse set about getting help from allies: Sigurd, earl of Orkney, who agreed to be in Dublin on Palm Sunday 1014; and two Viking leaders from the Isle of Man, Brodar and Ospak.

Brian and Mael Seachnaill were marching to Dublin when a dispute arose between them and Mael Seachnaill took

no part in the battle. Battle was joined at Clontarf on Good Friday 1014 and, although Brian was killed, his forces were victorious.

Clontarf became the subject of saga and storytelling in Irish and Norse tradition. Terrible portents and visions were said to

have been seen by both sides on the eve of the battle: a fairy woman appeared to Brian's followers and foretold disaster; Saint Senan also appeared, demanding compensation for an attack on a monastery years before. In the Isle of Man there were ghostly assaults on Brodar's ships, and ravens with iron beaks and claws attacked his followers.

While the battle of Clontarf was not a simple case of Irish against Norse, it signalled the end of the power of Norse Dublin and the effective end of the Viking Age in Ireland.

Expansion in Europe and Asia

The people of Great Britain and Ireland sometimes forget that the Vikings ventured much further than these shores. They left their mark on distant territories to the north, west, east and south of their Scandinavian homelands. The Americas, the Mediterranean and even Asia were within their compass, but one of Britain's much nearer neighbours also felt the marked influence of Norsemen.

When William of Normandy stepped onto England's south coast in 1066, he was doing more than seeking the crown he believed was rightfully his. He was following the example of his Viking forebears in venturing out in search of new lands and opportunity, to be seized by force of arms. Normandy took its name from that of the Viking invaders, who were called Normanni – men of the north.

The first Viking raids on the west coast of France began between 790 and 800 and some coastal areas were lost during the reign of the Frankish king Louis the Pious between 814 and 840. Scandinavians took advantage of confusion after Louis's death to make their first colony in Gascony, in the south-west. Assaults in 841 caused severe damage to Rouen and Jumièges and, as in Britain and elsewhere, the attackers sought out the treasures of the monasteries.

In 845 a Viking expedition up the Seine reached as far as Paris, and coins found in 1871 in Ireland probably came from raids in France between 843 and 846. After 851, Vikings began to winter in the lower Seine valley and twice more in the 860s rowed to Paris, leaving only when they acquired sufficient loot or bribes from the rulers of the Carolingian dynasty.

In 867, Charles the Bald signed the

Treaty of Compiègne, agreeing to yield the Cotentin peninsula to the Breton king Salomon on condition that the latter would fight as an ally against the Vikings. But in 911 the Viking leader Rollo forced Charles the Simple to sign a treaty under which Charles gave Rouen and the area of present-day Upper Normandy to Rollo, thus establishing the Duchy of Normandy. In return, in 940 Rollo pledged allegiance to Charles, agreed to be baptised and promised to guard the Seine estuaries against Viking attacks.

While many buildings including monasteries and abbeys were pillaged, burned, or destroyed by Viking raids, no French city suffered complete destruction. Rollo and his successors brought about rapid recoveries from the raids, however.

Most of the colonists were Danish, with a strong Norwegian element and a few Swedes. The merging of Scandinavians and French contributed to the creation of one of the most powerful feudal states of western Europe. The naval and military skills of the Normans, passed on from their Viking forebears, allowed them to conquer England and southern Italy and play a key role in the Crusades.

Meanwhile, Vikings had been busy in northern Europe for centuries, launching raids eastwards in search of wealth in the form of amber and furs, which were looted or taxed from the Finns, Wends, Slavs and others in the eastern Baltic region. Except for scattered raids, Russia was not subject to the Scandinavians' attentions until around 850.

The first evidence of incursions into Russia comes from the biography of Bishop Anskar of Hamburg, which relates how the Swedish king Olaf of Uppsala sent an army to punish a rebellious Latvian tribe and Danes in Lithuania. Soon afterwards a Scandinavian tribe called Rus appeared, and by 859 it had begun taxing the Slavs and Finns.

A typical advance began with armed traders detecting a lucrative source of goods and establishing fortified centres, with war bands in residence to protect their prizes. Settlement occurred around the garrisons, creating towns and trading cities, and once the peoples in one area had been pacified the process would be replicated further east.

Silver from mines in the Islamic regions of Tashkent and Afghanistan was the main lure for Scandinavian traders in Russia. The trade was centred at Bulghar or the Middle Volga, capital of the Northern Bulgar people who, because of the extensive silver trade they managed, became known as the Silver Bulgars.

Trade through Russia was difficult, in part because of hostile Slavic tribes; traders had to be as much warriors as businessmen. As a result, bands of Scandinavians who travelled eastwards joined together as companies, swearing oaths of mutual assistance, defence and support. The term for such an oath in Old Norse is *var*, and these adventurers became known as Varangians.

According to the Russian Primary Chronicle, the Rus were a group of Varangians, possibly of Swedish origin, who had a leader named Rurik. Rus is probably derived from the Finnish word for Sweden, which in turn comes from the Old Swedish *rother*, a word associated with rowing or ships, so *rothskarlar* meant 'rowers' or 'seamen'.

Leaders in Russia, disturbed by civil strife, invited Rurik and his followers to rule over them, according to the Chronicle: '... discord thus ensued among them, and they began to war one against another. They said to themselves: "Let us seek a prince who may rule over us, and judge us according to the law." They accordingly went overseas to the Varangian Rus: these particular Varangians were known as Rus, just as some are called Swedes, and others Normans, Angles and Goths, for they were thus named. The Chuds, the Slavs and the Krivichians then said to the people of Rus: "Our whole land is great and rich, but there is no order in it. Come to rule and reign over us." They selected three brothers, with their kinfolk, who took with them all the Rus, and migrated. The oldest, Rurik, located himself in Novgorod; the second, Sinaeus, in Beloozero; and the third, Truvor, in Izborsk. On account of these Varangians, the district of Novgorod became known as Russian (Rus) land. The present inhabitants of Novgorod are descended from the Varangian race, but aforetime they were Slavs.'

The Rus were in contact with Byzantium as early as 838, lacking the resources to raid the capital at Constantinople before then. The 838 date is supported by a Byzantine account that relates that a party of Swedish traders had to turn back because their way north up the Dnieper was blocked by 'savage tribes' – perhaps the Magyars.

In 860 the Normans, following a successful campaign in the Mediterranean, attacked Constantinople. Byzantine forces, particularly the fleet, were also occupied with a campaign against the Arabs to their east. This was the moment when the Rus launched their first assault against Miklagard, the Golden City, led by the Rus leaders Askold and Dir.

The Rus attack is best described in the

Greek sermons of the Patriarch Photius.
His sermon described the fury of the
attack, the terror of the Greeks and the
terrible loss of life and property outside

the city. Photius said the attack took the
Greeks completely by surprise, 'like a
thunderbolt from heaven'. He went on
to describe the Rus as a fierce and savage

launched the attack down the Dnieper from Kiev. Other accounts set the numbers of the attacking Rus force between 200 and 2,000 ships, but the 200 figure is most probably nearer the mark and the ships would have been small, a kind of hybrid between a dugout canoe and the clinker-built Viking vessel.

Although the Greeks were taken by surprise and Byzantium was poorly defended in the absence of the fleet with its deadly weapon of Greek fire, the Rus didn't take the city. Greek sources attribute this failure to a miracle brought about by the singing of hymns to the Virgin Mary and a procession around the city walls led by the Patriarch bearing the Virgin's robe. This apparently resulted in a huge storm that scattered the Rus forces. Russian sources tell us that the Rus returned to Kiev in ignominy, and it's possible any plunder gained in attacking the outlying areas of Byzantium was lost in the flight before the storm.

Between 864 and 867 a party of Rus was sent to the Byzantine emperor Basil I to negotiate peace, and many of the members of the party requested instruction in Christianity. Perhaps Greek claims of the miracle had impressed them. This marked the beginning of a period

tribe of barbarian people, completely unknown and insignificant until they became famous in this attack.

The account showed that the Rus

of amicable relationships between the Greeks and the Rus, and it was the point at which the latter began serving in the Byzantine army.

Meanwhile, the failed Rus captains Askold and Dir were put to death by Oleg, the Rus ruler of Novgorod and foster father of Rurik's son Igor, and Oleg became ruler in Kiev as well as in Novgorod. With this consolidation of power he acquired the wherewithal to launch his own attack on Byzantium in 907.

When Oleg's forces arrived in the Golden Horn they found the sea lanes shut by a great chain closing the mouth of the Horn. The Rus slaughtered the Greek garrison, mounted their ships on wheels or rollers and let the wind carry them overland to reach the Bosphorus, and so arrive at the city. If we are to believe the Russian Primary Chronicle, the Greeks tried to feed poisoned food to Oleg and his men – an offer they refused – then promised to pay tribute to the Rus leader. Oleg demanded silk sails for his ships and linen sails for those of his allies, along with wine, gold and fruit. The Chronicle also claims that Oleg hung his shield over the city gate as a sign of victory.

Unfortunately, there is no corroboration from Greek sources of this attack, and it's widely believed the story was made up, using the details of previous raids on Byzantium, in an attempt to create a 'hero tale' glorifying Oleg. Another possibility is that a small raid was magnified into a major victory.

In 907 and again in 911, the Byzantines negotiated trade treaties with the Rus that put an end to excursions against their city for many years. The next attack recorded by the Primary Chronicle is in 941, and it was an assault led by Igor, son of Rurik and foster son of Oleg. Unlike the account of the 907 attack, this one is corroborated by Liutprand, later Bishop of Cremona – his stepfather had witnessed the 941 attack.

The Greeks met this threat by equipping a number of older ships and galleys with Greek fire projectors. The Byzantine historian and princess Anna Komnene, writing around 1148, gave some clues about the nature and use of this mysterious and devastating weapon: 'This fire is made by the following arts. From the pine and certain such evergreen trees inflammable resin is collected. This is rubbed with sulphur and put into tubes of reed, and is blown by men using it with violent and continuous breath. Then in this manner it meets the fire on the tip and

πῦρρικῶν. ἡρωσδὲ καὶ τοοσκ‌λαφιὼπρωσολωΐπυρι

φολεερωμων πυρπολ   τὸν τῶνέηληπσλον

catches light and falls like a fiery whirlwind on the faces of the enemies.'

When the fleets met the seas were calm, perfect for the use of Greek fire, and many Rus threw themselves into the sea to drown rather than face the flames. Only those who managed to get their ships to the shore quickly survived; the Greek ships, of deeper draught, could not follow them into the shallows. A number of captured Rus were beheaded publicly.

In 944 Igor returned with another fleet, including an army of Slavs and Pechenegs – Turkic people from the Central Asian steppes. The emperor, hearing word of the attack, offered to pay the Rus tribute. The Rus then turned to attack Arabs in the area of the Caspian Sea, but a large number were either poisoned, as described by Arabic sources, or, more probably, fell victim to a virulent disease that devastated their forces.

Legend has it that the Rus dynasty founded by Rurik endured until 1598, when Fedor, the son of Ivan IV, died without an heir.

Above: *Greek fire, used to defeat the Rus*

New Worlds

Whatever the reasons for the Viking expansion as far south as north Africa and far east as Russia and the Middle East, they were probably the same as those that drove Scandinavians to explore and settle in the North Atlantic. These excursions resulted in the opening up of new worlds and the first known European contact with what we now know as North America.

The first new world to be settled was Iceland, and historians usually cite 874 as the year of the Scandinavians' first migration. The era of Icelandic settlement is generally accepted as having lasted until 930, when most of the island had been claimed and its assembly, the Althing, was established.

One historical source, a manuscript preserved on skin known as the Landnámábok, reveals that 435 men were the first settlers and that the first Norseman to set foot on Icelandic soil was a Viking called Naddoddr. He didn't stay long, but long enough to name the country Snaeland – the Land of Snow.

Naddoddr was followed by a Swede, Gardar Svavarsson. Some time around 860 his ship was driven by a storm far to the north until it reached Iceland's eastern coast. He sailed westward along the coast and then north, building a house on the north coast. Svavarsson sailed right round the island before leaving the following summer, but one of his men, Náttfari, stayed behind with two slaves and settled close – although not permanently – to Skjálfandi.

The next Norseman to arrive in Iceland – we don't know exactly when – was Flóki Vilgerdarson, who landed in the Westfjords after passing what is now

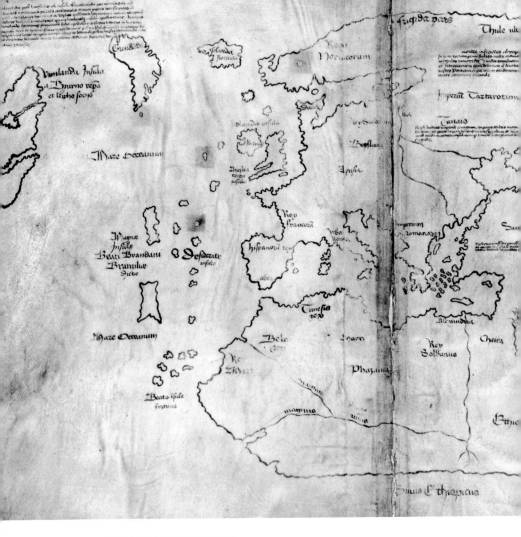

Left: *Map of Vinland as settled by Leif Erikson. Photo Yale University Press*

Reykjavik. A harsh winter caused all of his cattle to die and, cursing the country, he decided to name it Ísland – Iceland. Despite difficulties in finding food, he and his men stayed another year before heading back to Norway the following summer. Flóki would return much later to settle.

Another Norseman, Ingólfur Arnarson, and his foster-brother Hjörleifur went on an exploratory expedition to Iceland and stayed for a winter, returning a few years later to settle the land with their men. When they approached the island, Arnarson threw his high seat pillars overboard and swore he would settle where they drifted to land. When summer came, Arnarson built a farmstead in Reykjavik and claimed a large portion of land.

The age of settlement in Iceland is considered to have begun with his arrival, for he was the first to voyage to Iceland with the intention of settling. But he was followed by many others, and within about 60 years all the usable land had been taken. Sources mention 1,500 farm and place names as well as more than 3,500 people. It is difficult to tell the number of migrants to the island during the age of settlement, but scholars reckon it was between 15,000 and 20,000.

Long after the Icelandic age of settlement had ended – in around 986 – Norsemen colonised two areas along Greenland's south-west coast, even though the land was far from ideal for farming. The settlers arrived during a warm phase, when short-season crops such as rye and barley could be grown, and sheep and cattle were also raised for food, wool and hides. The settlers' main export was walrus ivory, which was traded for iron and other goods.

Greenland became a dependency of the king of Norway in 1261. The population may have reached as many as 5,000 during the 13th century, and it was divided between two main settlements – an eastern one and one further north which nevertheless was known as the Western Settlement. The settlements consisted of around 250 farms divided into communities centred around 14 churches, one of which was a cathedral at Gardar.

As time went on the climate changed and in 1379 the northernmost settlement was attacked by Inuit people, who had arrived in Greenland in the 13th century. Crops failed, trade declined and the colony faded away. By 1450 it had lost contact with Norway and Iceland.

There is still a European population in Greenland, but compared to that in North America – another discovery of the Vikings – it is utterly insignificant. According to Erik the Red's Saga and the Saga of the Greenlanders, Norsemen began to explore to the west a few years after the Greenland settlements were established.

And in 985, while sailing from Iceland to Greenland with a fleet of ships conveying settlers, a merchant by the name of Bjarni Herjólfsson was blown off course and, after three days, sighted land to the west. He was only interested in finding his father's farm, but he described his discovery to Leif Erikson, Icelandic son of the Norwegian outlaw Erik the Red, born around 970. Erikson explored the area in more detail and established a small settlement 15 years later.

The sagas tell us that three areas were discovered during his exploration: Helluland ('land of the flat stones'), Markland ('land of forests', of interest to settlers in Greenland, where there were few trees); and Vinland, which we may translate as either 'land of wine' or 'land of meadows' and was somewhere south of Markland. The sagas describe how a settlement was established in Vinland.

Using information from Herjólfsson, and in the same ship the merchant had used, Erikson sailed westward for 1,800 miles with a crew of 35. He had wanted his father to lead the expedition, but as Erik attempted to join his son he fell off his horse and was forced by that bad omen to stay behind.

Erikson described Helluland as 'level and wooded, with broad white beaches wherever they went and a gently sloping shoreline.' He wintered in 1001, probably near Cape Bauld on the northern tip of Newfoundland, where one day his foster father was found drunk on what were described as 'wine-berries' – possibly squashberries, gooseberries or cranberries.

Leif spent another winter in Vinland before sailing back to Greenland. In 1004, his brother Thorvald sailed with a crew of 30 to Newfoundland and spent the following winter at Leif's camp. In the spring, Thorvald attacked nine local people who were sleeping under skin-covered canoes. One victim escaped and returned to the Norse camp with an armed party, and Thorvald was killed by an arrow that passed through the camp's defences.

Despite the hostilities, the Norse explorers stayed another winter and left the following spring. Another of Leif's brothers, Thorstein, sailed to the New World to retrieve his brother's body, but he stayed just one summer.

In 1009, Thorfinn Karlsefni supplied three ships with livestock and 160 men and women. After a cruel winter, he headed south and landed at Straumfjord, later moving to Straumsöy. Here, peaceful relations were established with indigenous people and the two sides exchanged furs and squirrel skins, milk and cloth.

One source states that a bull belonging to Karlsefni stormed out of a wood, alarming the natives who ran to their boats and rowed away. They returned three days later with catapults, hoisting on a pole a large, dark blue sphere about the size of a sheep's belly, which flew over the men's heads and made a terrible noise. The Norsemen retreated but Leif's pregnant half-sister, Freydis Eiriksdóttir, was unable to keep up with them. Freydis pulled one of her breasts out of her bodice and struck it with a sword. This appears to have frightened the natives, who fled.

We don't know why short-term Norse settlements in North America didn't become permanent, though it was probably in part because of hostile relations with the indigenous peoples. Nevertheless, it appears that sporadic voyages to Markland for timber and trade could have lasted as long as 400 years. Evidence for this conclusion includes the Maine Penny, a Norwegian coin from between 1067 and 1093 reportedly found in a native American site in Maine, and an entry in the Icelandic Annals from 1347 that refers to a Greenlandic vessel that arrived in Iceland while attempting to return from Markland with a load of timber.

For many centuries after the voyages of Columbus opened the Americas to European colonisation, it was unclear whether the Vikings' stories represented real voyages. The sagas were taken seriously in 1837, when a Danish antiquarian pointed out the possibility for Norse settlement. Winland was first mentioned in written sources in a work by Adam of Bremen of around 1075. It was not until the 13th and 14th centuries that the sagas of Icelanders were put into writing.

The debate was settled in the 1960s, when a Norse settlement was excavated at L'Anse aux Meadows in Newfoundland, but the locations of the lands described

in the sagas are still unclear. Historians identify Helluland with Baffin Island and Markland with Labrador, but the location of Vinland is more difficult to establish. Most believe that L'Anse aux Meadows

is the Vinland settlement; others argue that the sagas depict Vinland as warmer than Newfoundland and must have been farther south.

But in 2012, possible signs of Norse outposts on Baffin Island and elsewhere were identified by researchers. Unusual fabric cordage found on Baffin was identified in 1999 as possibly of Norse manufacture. The Norse were there first.

Religion and Culture

Few aspects of the Vikings' lives have excited as much interest as their religious beliefs, and few have caused so much misunderstanding as their attitude towards Christianity. Did they attack churches and abbeys like the one on Lindisfarne out of a deep-rooted hatred of the Christian faith? Almost certainly not. Did their pagan upbringing give them a natural antipathy to the Christian God? Again, the answer is no.

The fascinating pantheon of gods to which the Scandinavians were devoted has long inspired storytellers, historians and film-makers. Just as interesting is the story of the way the Vikings took the Christian God to their hearts. At the beginning of the Viking Age, most of the population of Scandinavia was pagan, but the arrival of the Christian God meant that, for many, He could simply be added to the many deities they already had. And it's thought that the many Viking attacks on Christian religious institutions outside Scandinavia had more to do with those institutions' wealth and poor defences – making them easy targets – than any antipathy to the followers of Christ.

The fact that many Vikings, once they had come into contact with Christianity on their excursions overseas – in Ireland, the British Isles and Normandy, for example – accepted the faith can be verified by archaeological evidence. While grave goods were interred along with the deceased in pagan burials, Christians never took to this practice, so it is relatively simple to determine when a switch in belief systems took place.

But it wasn't only overseas that Vikings converted to Christianity: missionaries from Germany and the British Isles were

Above: *Detail of image of Norse gods Thor, Odin and Frey. Photo Berig*

busy in Scandinavia, and by the middle of the 11th century they had managed to establish Christianity in Denmark and most of Norway. Sweden took a little longer, hanging on until the 12th century before Christianity was well and truly established.

A fine example of aspects of one religion merging with those of another can be seen in Gamle Uppsala, Sweden. Here, vast pagan burial mounds sit cheek by jowl with the remains of an old church

– one religion had simply taken over the site of another.

There is a problem in learning about the pagan practices of the Vikings: there is very little evidence from the time to rely on, and while there are references to paganism in the Icelandic sagas, it should be borne in mind that they were mostly composed in the 13th century, 200 years or more after the establishment of Christianity among the Vikings in Scandinavia and beyond. What little we know about the Vikings' practices confirms that they sometimes involved the sacrifice of horses, and that chieftains combined that role with those of a kind of priest.

But we know a great deal more when it comes to the Vikings' gods. Early poems make reference to this pantheon and stories relating to the gods survived the conversion to Christianity in the form of myths rather than of religious beliefs. And it should be added that the stories make cracking reading and continue to inspire readers to this day.

The word Edda refers to a tale in both verse and prose that was written down in Iceland in the 13th century. The Eddas, in which the Vikings' pagan beliefs are presented in the form of folk tales, are our main source of knowledge about their beliefs. Here there is a wealth of information about the gods and how they interacted with the races of men, giants and dwarfs.

We know from the Eddas that the most powerful of the Vikings' gods was the one-eyed Odin, the Allfather of the gods and the ruler of Asgard, one of nine worlds and home to the gods. Odin was the god of wisdom and justice, of poetry and of war and death.

Within Asgard could be found the vast, majestic hall of Valhalla, again the domain of Odin. Half of those warriors who died in battle would be led to Valhalla by valkyries (from the Old Norse for 'chooser of the slain') while the other half would go the field of the goddess Freyja known as Fólkvangr. Once they had arrived in Valhalla, the dead would, in between feasting, prepare to aid Odin during Ragnarök – the great battle that would result in the death of the gods, a great fire and the submersion of the world in water. Fortunately for us, the myth states that just enough gods and giants survived Ragnarök for them to be able to build a new world.

It is interesting to note parallels between the myth of Odin and the

Opposite: *The great battle of Ragnarök, by Johannes Gehrts*

Christian story of the crucifixion and resurrection of Jesus Christ. According to the myth, Odin was sacrificed by being hanged on a tree and his side was pierced by a spear. His death, like that of Christ, was followed a few days later by his resurrection.

Frey was the god of fertility and prosperity and his twin sister Freyja was also worshipped as a fertility goddess, but in the Eddas she was often also shown as a goddess of love, beauty and attraction. The best loved and renowned goddess in the pantheon, Freyja was also associated with war, death, magic and prophecies. She rode in a chariot pulled by huge blue cats, or on a golden boar.

Thor is perhaps the best remembered god, not least for the fact that Thursday is named after him. (Other Norse gods are remembered in days of the week: Tyr in Tuesday, Odin in Wednesday and Odin's wife Frigg in Friday.) Overwhelmingly strong but rather stupid, the red-headed Thor was the god of thunder and the defender of gods and men from the giants. Dwarfs had crafted his magical war hammer Mjolnir, with which he slew giants and caused thunder. Usefully, Mjolnir would, after being thrown, return to its owner.

As you may guess from the preceding paragraphs, the giants were the great enemies of the gods and there were frequent conflicts between the two parties. Thor was the only god who could match the giants' strength, so the gods would often turn to the fire god Loki when they were in need of cunning to defeat their foes. Unfortunately for them, the mischievous, shape-shifting Loki, just like fire, was as liable to cause problems for the gods as he was to solve them.

Despite the frequent warring between gods and giants, there were occasional lessenings of tensions and liaisons between them. Loki, the son of a frost giant, was a prime mover in this regard, siring three monstrous children by his giantess wife. The myth says that as punishment for insulting the gods in a poem, Loki was bound to a rock with the intestines of one of his sons, there to await Ragnarök.

Loki's daughter, Hel, became the ruler of the underworld that bore the same name, from which we get our word Hell. His son Jörmungund was a sea serpent cast into the ocean by Odin, where he grew so huge that he could encircle the Earth and grasp his own tail.

Loki's other son, Fenrir the giant wolf, was tied up with a magical chain by the gods but freed himself from his bonds to kill and eat Odin at Ragnarök.

Besides their beliefs in gods, goddesses, giants and all manner of other supernatural beings, the Scandinavian peoples were steadfast in their belief in the power of witchcraft, and it may be that they were under the influence of a kind of Norse shamanism or sorcery called seidr. Practitioners of seidr, who could be of either gender although it was regarded as a rather unmanly practice, may have been believed to take visionary journeys. Archaeological evidence to support the existence of such shamans includes grave goods such as metal and wooden staffs, silver chair-shaped amulets and animal masks.

A grave discovered at a ring fort at Fyrkat in Denmark contained evidence, according to some experts, of the burial of a witch or sorceress from the Baltic region. The woman's coffin was a wagon and she was buried not with the usual pair of brooches but with silver rings on two of her toes. The grave goods interred with her included a bronze bowl containing fruit, two drinking horns, traces of a wooden staff, an iron spit and several amulets including one in the form of a chair. The list of grave goods goes on: a sheepskin pouch that probably contained henbane seeds (which were often used in 'magic brews') and a drinking glass. At the woman's feet was a locked oak box containing clothes, a pair of shears, a slate whetstone, a pottery spindle whorl, the lower jaw of a young pig and some owl pellets. Interpret that little lot as you will.

Comforted by their gods and goddesses, the Vikings nevertheless came under pressure to convert to Christianity – rendering relations more peaceful – as they ventured into the Frankish lands and the British Isles. A good example of a Viking converting and simultaneously furthering his career came with the Treaty of Wedmore in 878, when the warlord Guthrum accepted Christianity on King Alfred's terms and became ruler of East Anglia in turn.

Obstacles to the convention under which Christians were forbidden to trade with pagans were often overcome by means of a halfway house – the primsigning (first-signing). By showing a willingness to accept Christianity while not going the whole hog and undergoing Baptism, Scandinavian traders were deemed to be acceptable for the selling or buying of wares.

As Vikings settled in new homes and intermarried with local people, inevitable tensions between Christianity and paganism arose: should the children of such a marriage be brought up according to the dictates of the Christian faith? Further intermarriage eased the pressures gradually, and as the Church brought its influence to bear, complete conversions of families took place. It is possible to see how pagans lived peacefully alongside Christians from coins discovered in excavations of Viking York. One type of coin bears the name of the Christian Saint Peter, but on many of them the 'i' of Petri is in the form of a potent Norse symbol – Mjolnir, Thor's magical hammer.

Well before the Viking settlement of York, and even before the Viking Age, missionaries had journeyed to Scandinavia intent on conversion, with mixed results. It seems that their success rate in converting a populace was dependent on whether the local chieftain accepted Christianity or not. In the middle of the 10th century King Hakon the Good of Norway, who had been grown up in England having been fostered by the English King Athelstan,

attempted to use his regal power to impose Christianity on his subjects. It appears the chieftains were reluctant to abandon their beliefs, however, and Hakon gave up.

A more successful kingly attempt at conversion in the 10th century came from a king of Denmark and Norway, Harald 'Bluetooth' Gormsson. Apparently baptised by a monk named Poppa, Bluetooth is commemorated in runic inscriptions found on the Jelling stones in Norway. Here it is stated not only that he won the whole of Denmark and Norway but also that he 'turned the Danes to Christianity'. The Church's influence in Denmark became even more firmly established when Cnut ascended the thrones of both that country and of England.

Christianity had more trouble in establishing itself in Norway and Sweden in the 10th century, despite the best efforts of various missionaries. The conversions of Olaf Tryggvason, king of Norway from 995 to 1000, and Olof Skötkonung, who reigned in Sweden between 995 and 1022, had little impact on their subjects. But there followed the work of Saint Olaf, king of Norway from 1015 to 1028, which met with

more success and led to the eventual conversion of the country. The Swedes, among whom there was a pagan reaction against Christianity in the middle of the 11th century, held out longer. The Church of Rome had to wait for the 12th century before it could call Sweden its own.

Above: *Loki Bound, by WG Collingwood*

Life with the Vikings

Perhaps it doesn't capture the imagination quite like the vicious Viking raids that terrorised large parts of Europe for so many years, or the intrepid explorations that opened up new worlds and new trade routes, but the daily life of early medieval Scandinavians has plenty to enthral.

What were they really like when they took off their helmets and hung up their weapons? How did Viking family life differ from our own, or from that of other peoples of their time? What did they eat? How did they dress? What were their houses like? How did they relax after a hard day's raiding? Who created their art, and why?

We should start by taking a look at the structure of Scandinavian society of the Viking Age, which consisted of three classes of people: jarls, or chieftains;

karls, or free peasants or farmers; and thralls, as slaves were known – the word literally meant 'unfree servant'.

The jarl – the word is linked to our 'earl' – was a lordly warrior who ruled over a region with the aid of his armed followers. As the Viking Age wore on, the countries of Scandinavia we know today began to take on their early shapes and the jarls, losing some of their jealously kept independence, began to take orders from a king. But in practice the jarl was often still the lord of all he surveyed within his own domain.

Karls formed the next stratum of Viking society. Although they were free in name, they might have a duty of service to their chieftain, or they might hire themselves out for work on a farm or in a household to a wealthier landowner from their own class. The

LITTLE BOOK OF **VIKINGS**

karls, when they weren't being farmers, craftsmen or landowners, also formed the hordes of armed followers whom the chieftains recruited to launch raids and other expeditions.

The lowest of the low in Scandinavian society was the thrall, whose life held little or no value. As many as 30 of these unhappy souls might slave on a farm of reasonable size for no reward other than meagre rations. It was possible, however, for a thrall to buy his freedom by paying his owner his current worth if he had some way of raising the cash. Words of caution here: the use of the pronouns 'his' and 'he' should not be interpreted as meaning that thralls were exclusively male – far from it.

The three classes were thought to have been created by the god Rig or Heimdall, the father of mankind, and the Vikings believed that he created the thralls first. Nevertheless, the thralls' destiny was to be the property most commonly traded by Vikings. Slaves snatched from a foreign land (or even from a neighbouring one; Scandinavians weren't above raiding their cousins for a few thralls) would be brought to market where merchants would barter for the most desirable specimens, whether they

Left:
Reconstruction of Erik the Red's house. Photo Wolfgang Sauber

came from far-off Byzantium or nearby Sweden.

The purchased slave faced a life as grim as that of one who had been born into slavery – or that of the karl who had been reduced by bankruptcy to thraldom, or had found himself a thrall as punishment for a crime. Their owners were entitled to sacrifice a thrall to the gods or beat him to death for the tiniest transgression. Even if he escaped death, the thrall was forced to perform the heaviest and filthiest tasks: building walls, spreading manure, herding pigs and goats, digging peat, for example. It was the job of female thralls to grind corn and salt, do the milking, churning and washing and sometimes act as the master's partner in bed.

It was easy to tell who was a thrall and who was not. They were the ones wearing slave collars round their necks and the simplest of tunics. They were the ones whose hair was cropped short. They were the ones whose names – Clumsy, Hunchback, Torn-Skirts – betrayed their lowly status. The child of a slave was always a slave and, while an owner was obliged to provide a living and medical care for thralls who were injured in their service, most could not

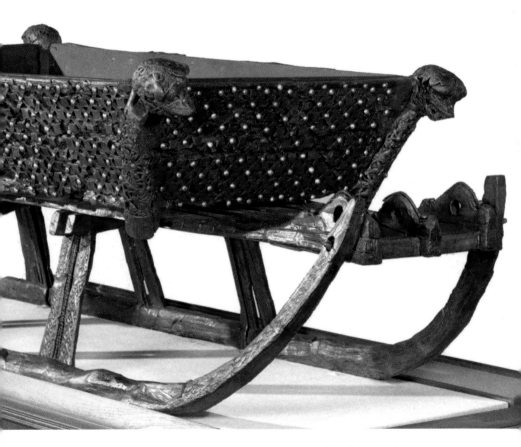

own property or get married. Their children were the property of their owners.

There was occasionally some relief: male thralls, if they were favoured by their masters, could become a bailiff or a valet. An owner might allow a thrall to work a small parcel of land and pocket the proceeds, and they were entitled to sell any crafts they produced in their free time. Thus a thrall might accumulate enough money to buy his freedom.

Sometimes thralls might even be freed by their owners as a reward for loyal service; sometimes their freedom might be bought by a third party. The freed man would be adopted into his master's family and given the rights and duties of any other free person in the law. One of the sagas relates the tale of an Icelandic slave named Asgaut, a big, capable man who had few equals among the ranks of the free-born. Asgaut was rewarded for his exemplary and loyal service by being granted his freedom and a gift of money, whereupon he left Iceland for Denmark, where he established a reputation as a man of courage.

In comparison to the life of the thrall, that of the master was a bed of roses. In a wealthy household he would sit at table on a high seat flanked by carved wooden pillars, surrounded by his adoring family. The concept of family was highly important in Viking society, and it was a man's duty to serve the family group with dedication. If he let his kin down, he risked being cast out.

Marriages were often arranged by parents or grandparents, for the union was as much between families as it was between the happy couple. And woe betide the married person who abused the alliance with a little dalliance: the penalty for adultery was death for the man and being sold into slavery for the woman. Likewise, death was the punishment for the rape of a virgin. Still, the Viking menfolk's liaisons with concubines or foreign slaves were often tolerated. The typical Viking male, on the other hand, showed immense respect for women, unlike many contemporaries. It all made for a comfortable home life.

What were their homes like? The Vikings were, as we've seen, farming people whose life was based around the farmstead, which would typically consist of a group of houses, stables, barns, boathouses and a smithy. The community's well would be wood-lined and the farmstead would also feature wood in pathways of tightly packed logs that sometimes connected the buildings.

Houses were also built from wood, sometimes resting on a row of stones to prevent the incursion of damp. There were various methods of construction, including the log cabin type, in which walls were built of horizontal logs jointed at the ends, and another kind in which vertical or horizontal planks were attached to corner posts. The size of the building depended on the length of the tree trunks available in the vicinity. Walls were sometimes filled in with wattle and daub – thin branches or reeds plastered with mud or clay.

The word 'longhouse' is usually associated with Scandinavian dwellings of the Viking period. Houses were indeed oblong in shape, either rectangular or with curved walls, and their roofs were thatched with straw or reeds. Sometimes, in an attempt to keep a house warm, farmers would roof it with turf and allow the grass to keep growing.

The interior of the longhouse would be, at first sight, simple. This was a single room within which the entire family would eat, sleep, work and amuse themselves and their friends – the duty of hospitality was highly important in Scandinavian society. And it would have been a room that was dark, smelly and smoky, for there was no chimney through which the smoke from the large fireplace could escape. The most important members of the family would have their sitting and sleeping places nearest the fire, while others would sit and sleep on benches or fur-covered earth platforms around the room. Servants and slaves? They would have to make do well away from the fire, or even in a byre with animals.

Vikings don't seem to have been much concerned with lighting their homes – there were no books to read, after all – as there were often no windows. Glass was unheard of, but sometimes a longhouse might feature a small opening at a gable end, covered with a stretched pig's bladder or a calf's birth membrane. Otherwise, the only light came from oil lamps or wax candles. Combined with fumes from the fire they would have contributed to a terrible fug, and some experts believe that some Vikings suffered from carbon monoxide poisoning.

As for the longhouse's furniture – well, there wasn't much to speak of. We

know from archaeological excavations that the better off Viking might sleep on an ornately carved bed complete with a mattress stuffed with feathers and down, but this was a luxury unavailable to most. A few low stools might be scattered about and there might have been wooden chests in which valuables were stored, but chairs were rare. Tools, weapons, pots and pans, sacks and buckets were hung from hooks on the walls.

The floor of a longhouse was composed of compacted earth, or sometimes wooden planks, over which straw was laid. The lack of sophistication applied to waste disposal and toilet arrangements too: waste was tipped

outside the house and toilets were little more than a hole in the ground. Moss might come in handy as a cleansing tool. This is not to say the Vikings were dirty people, despite the popular image. A bath-house could sometimes be found among the outbuildings, and Sunday is known to have been washing day. Early saunas were improvised by throwing water on heated stones to create clouds of cleansing steam.

Vikings are known to have usually eaten two meals a day: the first, the 'day meal', was taken about two hours after the start of the day's work (around seven or eight in the morning); and the second, the 'night meal', was consumed when work had finished, perhaps at seven or

Right: *Oseberg ship at the Museum of Cultural History, University of Oslo, Norway*

eight in the evening.

The Vikings' meat-derived protein was derived from beef, mutton, lamb, goat, pork or horsemeat. The importance of cattle to their society can be gauged from archaeological investigations that have found farms with space for up to 100 animals, and from the fact that the Old Norse word for money had a root meaning of 'cattle'. Slaughter of the animals was mainly carried at the end of the grazing season, and farmers had to assess their hay supplies carefully and decide how many – and which – animals could be kept through the winter. Viking people also kept chicken, geese and ducks for eggs and meat.

Various methods of meat preservation, including drying, smoking, salting, fermentation, pickling in whey, or even freezing in northern Scandinavia, were used. Fermentation of meat – still used for some Scandinavian delicacies – was often accomplished by covering the unopened animal in a pit and leaving it to ferment.

The amount of meat from wild animals eaten by the Vikings was low compared to that from domestic sources, but in the northernmost areas game represented a larger proportion of the meat consumed. Deer, elk, reindeer and hare were hunted for meat, as were bear, boar and squirrel. In Viking areas of England, wild birds used for food included plovers, black grouse, woodpigeon and lapwing.

Nuts were another source of protein, but it's estimated that up to a quarter of the calories in the diet of coastal Norwegians of the Viking era came from fish. Even Norwegians who lived inland had access to high proportions of fish, and in eastern Scandinavia herring, haddock, ling and mackerel formed an important part of the diet. There is also evidence that a variety of freshwater fish – like roach, rudd, bream, perch and pike – and shellfish were eaten. The dry, cold conditions in northern Scandinavia allowed fish to be preserved almost indefinitely by drying.

Beached whales were another important food source for Vikings, and the sagas often mention disputes over the legal rights of a landowner to the meat, blubber and bone. The mammals were also trapped in inlets with narrow openings, where they were driven aground from boats or shot with poisoned arrows. Porpoises and seals were hunted, too.

Fruit, often preserved by drying, was high on the Vikings' food agenda. They might treat themselves to sloes, plums, cherries, bullaces (an early

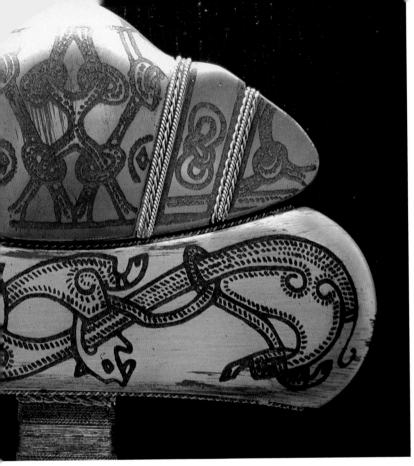

form of damsons), apples, blackberries, bilberries, raspberries, elderberries, hawthorn berries, cloudberries, strawberries, crabapples, rosehips and rowanberries. Scandinavians also grew or gathered vegetables such as carrots, parsnips, turnips, spinach, wild celery, cabbage, radishes, beans, peas beets, leeks, onions and seaweed, and mushrooms were often sought after.

Milk from cows and goats was not usually drunk but was used to make foods that could be stored for the winter, such as butter, buttermilk, whey, curds and cheese. Whey was used either as a drink or as a preservative to pickle meat and fish.

Archaeologists sometimes find the remains of cereal grains or bread at Viking Age sites. Barley was the most commonly grown grain in Sweden and Denmark and rye began to be grown in Finland and parts of Sweden and Denmark around 1000 to 1200. In Norway, oats and barley were grown and wheat has also been found. Barley was used for thin, flat bread, baked on an open fire, and in Denmark it was used primarily for porridge and beer. It's thought that rye became the main bread cereal in southern Scandinavia during the Viking Age.

Most of the barley would have been used to make ale. Porridge or gruel was an important everyday food for the Viking farm family. During the week the grain would be cooked in water, but for celebrations porridge would be cooked with milk and eaten with butter.

Some loaves are believed to have been baked on a slab or iron pan; ovens were rare. The hand-mill used to grind flour consisted of a flat, stationary stone with another on top, the top stone being turned by a handle fixed at the edge and pierced in the middle, where the raw material to be ground was introduced. Turning a mill was heavy work, and almost always reserved for thralls.

The Vikings used herbs and spices in their cooking, among them dill, coriander, hops, poppy seed, mustard, fennel, watercress, cumin, mustard, horseradish, lovage, parsley, mint, thyme, marjoram, caraway, juniper berries and garlic. Vinegar and honey were used as flavourings.

When it came to alcoholic drinks the Vikings were enthusiastic consumers of ale flavoured with hops and bog myrtle. Mead, using honey grown in southern regions, was another favourite and a drink that was both very alcoholic and sweet was bjórr. Fruit wines were used for sacramental purposes, and grape wine was imported from the Rhine by the wealthy.

Cooking, strictly the province of women, was carried out using utensils surprisingly like those of today and a fireplace or hearth called the meal-fire, which was built near mealtime. The men were responsible for the hunting and slaughtering of animals for meat. The sagas tell us that sometimes women had to stay up all night to finish cutting up meat, which was usually boiled, often in clay or soapstone pots.

What did Scandinavian people wear during the Viking Age? That depended to a great extent on what social class they belonged to. The style and cut of a man's or woman's outfit, the materials used and the quality of the pins that held it in place were clear indications of the owner's wealth and status.

Clothes pins made of metal have been found in many Viking graves and settlements but the material that clothing was made from has, naturally, proved much harder to find; the textiles haven't managed to survive. But experts have learned a little about the materials used in Viking Age clothing from small fragments that have managed to beat the ravages of time. The best evidence comes from some bundles of discarded fabric that were found preserved in the mud of Hedeby port, on the Danish-German border. The materials appear to have been used as packing material or perhaps for the tarring of ships. The find also shed some light on the tailoring methods used by the Vikings.

The outer garment for the man's upper body was the overtunic, made from wool using surprisingly complicated patterns, with many pieces cut out of the fabric and sewn back together. The skirt of the tunic ranged from thigh- to knee-length and, as with most items of clothing, the length was determined by the wealth of the owner. A poorer man wouldn't waste material that wasn't needed, while a better off individual would show off his wealth by using more material than was needed. On hot days, the skirt was lifted up and tucked into the belt. Sleeves were probably longer than in modern garments, reaching well past the wrists. Men's necklines were high, for revealing the chest was considered effeminate.

The tunics of all but the poorest people were decorated with braid on the neckline and cuffs and, for the more wealthy, on the hem of the skirt. The braid was woven from brightly coloured wool.

A wide range of styles of trousers was used in Scandinavia: some were tight while others were baggy; some trousers were of simple construction while

Magtens guld

"Et bæger blev ham b...

others were more complicated, using gores around the crotch for freedom of movement and built-in socks, with belt loops around the waist. Trousers had neither pockets nor fly, meaning that men had to pull up their tunic skirts and drop their trousers to relieve themselves.

The cloak was simply a large, rectangular piece of wool, sometimes lined with wool of a contrasting colour. It was typically worn offset, with the right arm – the one that held a weapon – free and unencumbered. Cloaks could be embroidered or trimmed with braid and typically hung to somewhere between the knee and the ankle, depending on the wealth of the owner.

Scandinavian women wore multiple layers of ankle-length clothing, made of both wool and linen. These would be held in place by a pair of brooches, one on each shoulder. The brooches were usually oval-shaped but styles varied from region to region. Women would also often have a third brooch, which would sit near the neck, and sometimes glass or amber beads or other jewellery was strung between brooches.

Women almost always wore head coverings, sometimes as simple as a knotted kerchief. A number of different kinds of head coverings mentioned in the sagas seem to have been elaborate head-dresses that may have been worn on special occasions, and it has been suggested that types of head-dress served to distinguish married from unmarried women.

Viking shoes were made of a large piece of leather sewn into the shape of the user's foot and usually secured by leather straps. Today's shoe industry bosses would be horrified to learn that there does not appear to have been much difference in shoe styles between the sexes; footwear seems to have been about function rather than style. Wealthier people would have worn coarse, heavy woollen socks, while perhaps those who could not afford such luxuries tried to keep their feet warm by stuffing their shoes with dried grass or moss.

It seems long hair was favoured by both sexes – unless you happened to be a thrall, in which case your hair was cut short. Some men shaved their hair or had it rolled in a tight bun near the nape of the neck, while some women teased their hair into a complicated series of knots on the crown of the head. The sheer number of combs found in excavated sites suggests the Vikings

LIFE WITH THE VIKINGS

were very concerned about their hair. Combs, of course, could have been used to control lice, but it's clear that hairstyles were highly important, and men would often have finely groomed beards and moustaches.

It was essential for Vikings to relax properly after a hard day on the farm or raid. Luckily, they seem to have had a wide range of board games and sports to help them do just that.

Game boards found among grave goods have playing surfaces ranging from seven x seven up to 19 x 19 squares. Playing pieces were made from a wide variety of materials: glass, bone, antler, amber, bronze and wood. Dice have also been found, but a medieval Icelandic law book made it clear that gambling on dice or board games was prohibited. In the stories, some of the playing pieces are described as having long pins that fitted into the board.

One board game was called, unfortunately for English speakers, hnefatafl. We don't know the rules, but it appears to have been a strategy game in which a king and his retainers opposed a much larger army. Pawns might be made from the teeth of marine mammals while the king might be fashioned from whalebone.

It is possible that Viking people learned shatranj, an early form of chess, through their trading contacts in Constantinople. In one of the sagas two men played a board game that ended in mate, which suggests that the game was chess. Carved walrus ivory game pieces found on the Isle of Lewis in the Hebrides have long been interpreted as chess pieces made in Norway in the 12th century, when the island was under Norwegian rule.

Among the Vikings' favourite indoor pastimes were drinking games, for drinking to excess appears to have been common at feasts and other celebrations. People often drank in pairs, with an important man having a woman as his exclusive drinking partner for the evening.

One pastime consisted of pairs of men trading drinks and sparring with words. Participants were expected to compose a verse of poetry with each drink, bolstering their own reputation with boasts of courageous and manly behaviour while disparaging their opponents. Naturally, as the drinkers became less inhibited, the intensity of the insults and boasts would have

grown. The goal was to maintain one's verbal skill without showing the effects of alcohol. Another rowdy game played in the longhouse after the evening meal was hnútukast, in which players threw bones left over from the meal at each other, with the aim of causing an injury.

The sagas are full of references to Viking sports including ball games, wrestling, swimming (perhaps more accurately described as drowning; the goal was to see who could hold his opponent underwater the longest) and horse fights. Games, which were important social events and could last for days, took place when Scandinavians came together for feasts, assemblies, or religious festivals. And it is clear that serious injury and even death were not uncommon.

Knattleikr was played with a hard ball and a bat. We don't know the rules, the object of the game or the natures of the equipment or the playing field, but the sagas tell us it was played widely. It appears to have been a full contact sport in which players were held back and tackled, and disputes could turn very bloody indeed.

In Viking wrestling, which sometimes took place indoors, a win was claimed if a participant was thrown off his feet, or lifted clear and then dropped onto any part of his body except his feet. It's believed that grappling was an important element in combat, and it seems likely that wrestling contests were the means by which men kept their fighting skills honed.

Weightlifting competitions used heavy stones and another test of strength was toga hönk (tug of war). It's thought that two men sat on the ground, knees bent, with the soles of their feet pressed together, and heaved on a loop of rope in an attempt to pull the opponent over. As the sport used movements and muscle groups similar to those used in rowing, it's possible it was used to find capable rowers.

The playing of games appears to have been limited to Viking men; women were unlikely to attend, for instance, a horse fight, where violence seems to have been an inevitable outcome. But board games appear to have been played by both genders.

Viking children played with a variety of carved wooden toys, including dolls, horses and ships, and child-sized wooden weapons have also been found. Other toys are mentioned in the sagas; in one a six-year-old boy gives his bronze horse to a four-year-old, saying it would suit the younger child better.

We have seen the importance of the composition of poetry in Viking society. Poems that have survived show a wide range of topics and tones: sometimes respectful, sometimes boastful, humorous, threatening or obscene. Poems were thought to be a gift from Odin and had the power to bestow honour on a worthy man and to remove it from a wretch. A skilful poet could earn a valuable reward from a generous king, or save his life in the face of an angry ruler.

Poems praising a woman were banned because of the effect they might have on her reputation and the spell-binding effects they might have, but surviving love poems suggest the ban was ignored. And poems could have other unwanted outcomes: on hearing poetry implying that a man was womanish, that man was allowed to kill the poet.

If people in the Viking Age enjoyed music, they left little behind to prove it. Among the most convincing instruments that have been discovered is a 10th century bone flute found at Birka in Sweden, which is still playable today;

part of a 10th century set of wooden pan pipes found at York; and a ninth century amber bridge from a six-stringed instrument.

What's more, it seems that people of the Viking Age didn't create art for art's sake: there are very few examples of decorated objects having no purpose other than to display their ornamentation. Instead, Norse art is characterised by the extraordinary ornamentation of everyday objects. Even the humblest objects were elaborately decorated, many in ways that required high levels of skill.

And it has been pointed out that Norse poetry and literature had some of the same complexities as Norse art. In art, extremely complicated forms are used all over a figure to create a single, unified image; in literature, multiple plot lines are developed and abandoned, only to be taken up again in order to create a unified dramatic narrative. It's been suggested that this similarity between poetry and the visual arts stemmed from the same underlying sensibility in Norse culture: an appreciation and enjoyment of the ornate. The image of the Viking as a simple, thuggish brute could not be wider of the mark.

Truth or Fiction?

Over the centuries, stories about the Vikings have been embellished and grown taller, to the point at which fact has often been confused with fiction. Much has been misinterpreted, misread and even simply invented to please the entertainment industries and those hungry for thrills and gore. So how does everything we think we know about the Vikings stack up against the truth? Here are some home truths and some myths exploded.

Everyone knows that Viking warriors wore horned or even winged helmets, right? WRONG. Even though every so-called Viking helmet you can hire or buy in a fancy dress shop will feature upward-curving horns, there is simply no evidence that horned helmets were ever worn in battle during the Viking Age. Popular culture would have us believe they were

commonplace, but none have ever been found and they weren't depicted in any illustrations of the time.

How did this myth come about? Bronze Age Norse and Germanic priests, many centuries before the Viking Age, did sport horned headgear, and artists have sometimes been over-creative in plugging gaps in the historical record. The image seems to have been transplanted on to the Vikings by painters following the example of the costume designer Carl Emil Doepler, who introduced horned helmets for the first Bayreuth production of Wagner's Der Ring des Nibelungen in 1876.

The image of Viking raiders as smelly, unkempt brutes who never washed is WRONG. In fact it seems they were more scrupulous about their personal hygiene than other European peoples of

Above: *Viking helmets – but no horns. Photo Hans Splinter*

the time – including those in Britain.

Vikings, who were all for a dip in a natural hot spring when they could find one, were in the habit of bathing at least once a week, unlike many contemporaries. And they were in the habit of washing their faces and hands often. What's more, archaeological evidence indicates our Scandinavian friends used such aids to hygiene as razors, combs, tweezers and ear-cleaning spoons made from animal bones antlers or metal. Women often wore an ear spoon dangling from one of their brooches on a chain. We believe they made soap from horse chestnuts. However you criticise a Viking the next time you meet one, don't accuse him of uncleanliness.

The popular image of Viking warriors as huge, muscle-bound hulks is WRONG. While their basic anatomy was similar to ours, studies have shown that they were, on average, eight to 10 centimetres shorter than today's Scandinavians.

The short summers in the northern lands meant the raising of crops was difficult and food was scarcer than the ideal. While travellers sometimes brought different foods back from their travels, nutritional standards were low. With poor nutrition, children grew more slowly than those of the 21st century and usually simply didn't attain the size we are used to.

On the other hand, unrelenting hard work in the fields meant Viking bodies were probably more muscular than today's tend to be.

Have you heard the one about the nursery rhyme 'London Bridge is falling down' having a link to raiding Vikings? It is probably WRONG.

One theory about the origin of the rhyme refers to the destruction of the famous bridge by Olaf II of Norway in either 1009 or 1014. The story goes that Olaf was able to pull the bridge down into the Thames by attaching cables from his longships. And when the writer Samuel Laing translated the saga Heimskringla, a history of Norse kings, in 1844 he included a verse by the 11th century poet Óttarr svarti (Ottar the Black):

> London Bridge is broken down.
> Gold is won and bright renown.
> Shields resounding,
> War horns sounding.
> Hild is shouting in the din!
> Arrows singing
> Mail-coats ringing.
> Odin makes our Olaf win!

It looks convincing, but more recent translations have shown that Laing was very free in his translation and merely used the nursery rhyme as a model. It's not likely that this was an earlier version of the rhyme we learned as children. In fact, some historians are not even sure Olaf ever made an attack on the bridge, let alone pulled it down.

The notion that men held all the aces in Viking society and that their downtrodden women had no rights is WRONG. While it's true that girls could be married as young as 12 years and that women were left behind to tend home and farm while their husbands sailed off to glory, Norse women were actually better off than many at that time, and even later in history.

The womenfolk were in charge of

the keys to the longhouse and the thralls while the men were away on business. If they weren't thralls themselves they could inherit property, ask for a divorce – for reasons including the fact that a husband wore effeminate clothing, especially low-necked shirts exposing his chest – and reclaim their dowries if their marriages came to an end. (Incidentally, a man could divorce his wife if she dressed in men's trousers.)

That said, there's no getting away from the fact that if you were a female thrall, your life was unlikely to be a bed of roses.

Even to this day, the image of the Viking spending every waking hour raping, pillaging, burning and slaying persists. The idea that these activities took up all of their time is WRONG.

When they weren't travelling for one reason or another – and that reason might have been to trade with other peoples – many Viking men had their farms to look after. While raiding might have been lucrative sometimes, their families usually needed to be fed through other means.

There was often time for recreation, too. Vikings could avail themselves of a wide variety of physical pastimes such as skiing – there is evidence that

Scandinavian people were getting about on skis in about 5000BC – foot-racing, swimming and wrestling. And they had a number of board games, as the chessmen carved from walrus ivory, discovered on the Scottish island of Lewis, attest.

Famous Vikings

Their names echo down the centuries, sounding exotic to non-Scandinavian ears and promising tales of high adventure, derring-do and exploration. You don't need much imagination to understand how Eric Bloodaxe, Bjorn Ironside or Ingvar the Far-Travelled came by their soubriquets. On the other hand, the names of Ivar the Boneless and Ragnar Hairy Breeches probably need a little explanation. Here are some of the most celebrated Vikings of them all.

Ragnar Lodbrok, who was active in the ninth century, achieved fame, or notoriety, as one of the great Viking heroes whose legendary deeds were celebrated in the sagas.

Claiming descent from the father of the gods Odin, Ragnar 'Hairy Breeches' embarked on many raids in Britain and France and had made his reputation as a great warrior – and gathered great power and wealth – by the 840s. He is said to have enjoyed attacking Christians on their holy days, ensuring they were off guard and closeted in their churches. In 845 he undertook a daring raid on Paris, sailing up the river Seine and defeating the forces of the Carolingian king Charles the Bald. The sacking of Paris and other cities led eventually to Vikings being given land on the north coast in exchange for protection from other raiders – land that became known as Normandy.

Ragnar, the father of many famous sons including Ivar the Boneless and Halfdan Ragnarsson, was finally captured by the Anglo-Saxon king Aella, who had him thrown into a pit

FAMOUS VIKINGS

of snakes to die. The sons' revenge took the form of invasion of England.

Having said all this, it's disappointing to note that historians are not sure a single Ragnar ever existed. It's possible his legend grew from the stories of several Viking heroes and kings.

Ivar the Boneless seems definitely to have existed. Born around 794 and growing up to become a warlord of great power, he was described as a man of exceptional cruelty and ferocity. He was also reputed to have been a berserker.

There is much doubt about the reason for Ivar Ragnarsson's nickname. One theory suggests he might have suffered from osteogenesis imperfecta, or brittle bone disease; another that it may have been a euphemism for impotence. It is certainly recorded that Ivar dwarfed all his fellows and was an immensely powerful man.

With his brothers Halfdan and Ubbe, Ivar invaded East Anglia in 865, leading what the Anglo-Saxon Chronicle called the Great Heathen Army. The following year it was York's turn to fall to the conquering Vikings. Aella, the killer of Ivar's father, was put to death by means of the gruesome torture method of the blood eagle: the ribs of the victim were cut by the spine and broken so they resembled wings; the lungs were then pulled out through the wounds.

Ivar turned his pitiless attentions first to Mercia and then to Dublin and Scotland, leaving corpses scattered in his wake and making off with riches beyond counting. He is thought to have died in about 873. A mass grave discovered in Repton, Derbyshire in 1686 contained the skeleton of a nine-foot tall Viking warlord who had died a violent death. Could this be the grave of Ivar the Boneless and his followers?

Gardar Svavarsson was a Swedish man who is thought to have been the first Scandinavian to live in Iceland, albeit for just one winter.

During a voyage to the Hebrides off western Scotland some time in the 860s, Svavarsson's ship was caught in a storm and driven northwards to the coast of Iceland. He sailed round the coast, finding that he had circumnavigated an island, and went ashore to pass the winter at a place now called Húsavík. Returning to Sweden, he called the new land after himself: Gardarshólmi.

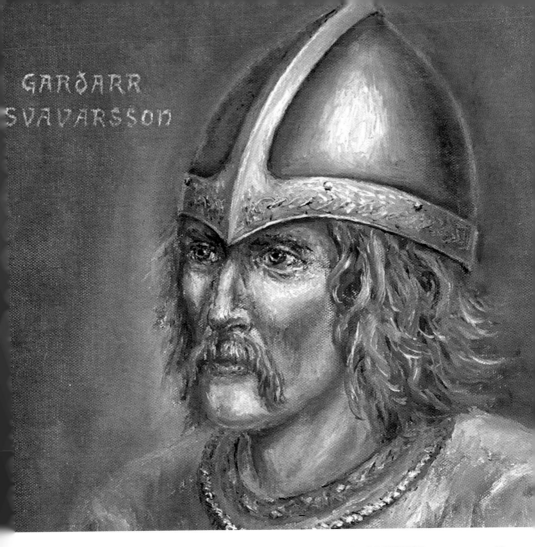

GARÐARR
SVAVARSSON

Eric Bloodaxe (c 885 – 954) started his piracy career at the early age of 12, it's said. By the time he died, he had reigned for a short time as king of Norway and twice as king of Northumbria.

The son of Norwegian king Harald Fairhair, Eric married Gunnhild, a daughter of the king of Denmark who was said to possess powers of sorcery. According to some sources, he was a bloodthirsty tyrant who had four of his brothers killed in order to keep the Norwegian crown on his head. Other evidence paints a picture of a more reasonable man who was chosen by the Northumbrians to be their king in 947.

When the English king Eadred invaded Northumbria, Eric's army encountered them at Castleford and 'made a great slaughter'. The people of Northumbria responded to Eadred's threats to destroy Northumbria in revenge by turning to him and away from Eric. But when Olaf Sihtricsson became the ruler instead, Eric drove him out and returned to the Northumbrian throne, only to be driven out in turn in 954. Eric's colourful reign was over.

Erik the Red, the founder of the first Norse settlement in Greenland, was born Erik Thorvaldsson in around 950, probably in western Norway. His nickname may have had something to do with his explosive temper as well as his hair and beard.

His family settled in Iceland after his father was banished for killing a man. Erik himself later served a three-year banishment from Iceland for murder and, after hearing of islands to the west, set sail with a crew in 982. Landing on Greenland's east coast, he then rounded the southern tip before landing again in the south-west and spending three winters exploring this region.

Returning to Iceland, Erik encouraged settlement of the land he called Greenland. In 486 he set sail with up to 500 prospective settlers and established an eastern settlement (Brattahlid) and one in the west (Godthab). Some settlers returned to Iceland while the rest disappeared, victims of either the Inuit people or disease or starvation. Erik died during the winter of 1003/04.

Leif Erikson (c 970 – c 1020) is regarded as the first European to set foot in North America, 500 years before Christopher Columbus.

The second son of Erik the Red, while in Norway he was asked by King Olaf I to spread Christianity to settlers in

Effigies Erici Rauderi ad delineatio=
nem Einarsi Eiolfsonü adumbrata

è Norvagia in Islandiam aufugit, ubi in promontorio ejus=
dem Insula caurum versus villam vocatam Drangar ad

Erikson's native Greenland. According to one version of the story, his ships got to Greenland but ran off course on the way back to Norway and the first dry land they found was in North America – probably today's Nova Scotia. Erikson named the new land Vinland, perhaps because of grapes his landing party found. Other versions have him travelling to Vinland on purpose, having heard of its existence from travellers who had already been there more than 10 years previously.

Erikson left his discovery behind after one winter and went home to concentrate on spreading the Christian message. One of his brothers, Thorvald, later revisited Vinland.

Sweyn Forkbeard (c 960 – 1014), son of the Danish king Harald Bluetooth and father of Cnut the Great, was a highly successful Viking warrior and king of several territories. Having rebelled against his father in 987 to secure the Danish throne, he was part of a trio of allies who defeated Olaf I of Norway about 1000, becoming virtual ruler of the country.

Turning to England, Sweyn led expeditions to exact revenge for the St Brice's Day massacre of Danes in 1002. He returned in 1013 with a successful campaign that forced Ethelred the Unready into exile and put Sweyn on the throne – the first Danish King of England. He died shortly afterwards, having ruled England for a mere five weeks.

Some Norse women achieved notoriety through the sagas. **Sigrid the Haughty**, if she ever lived – the matter is in some doubt – certainly lived up to her nickname.

One of the sagas tells us that Sigrid was a beautiful, powerful widow who did not take kindly to being wooed by the kings Harald Grenske and Vissavald of Gardarik. In order to discourage further suitors she had them burned to death in a great hall. Nevertheless, the king of Norway, Olaf Trygvasson, tried his luck, insisting that Sigrid convert to Christianity for them to be married. When she refused, Olaf hit her with a glove, leading Sigrid to threaten calmly: 'This may some day be thy death.'

She then worked towards Olaf's downfall, allying Sweden with Denmark by marrying his enemy Sweyn Forkbeard. Olaf married Sweyn's sister Tyri, who urged him into conflict with her brother, while Sigrid also goaded Sweyn into action. The result was the one-sided naval Battle of Svolder in 999 or 1000, during which Olaf flung himself into the sea in full armour rather than face death at his enemies' hands. Sigrid's revenge was complete.

The name of **Cnut the Great**, better known to many as Canute, is remembered mainly as the ruler who commanded the sea's waves to turn back to show that his power was as nothing compared to that of God. There was more to him than demonstrations of humility.

Born between 985 and 995, the son of Sweyn Forkbeard, Cnut was victorious over Edmund, King of England, at Ashingdon in 1016, giving him control of the Danelaw and the Midlands. Edmund's death shortly afterwards meant Cnut became the first Viking king of all England. Two years later his brother Harald, King of Denmark, died, leaving Cnut to rule that country, and two years after that he added Norway to his growing empire. By the late 1020s, having secured the submission of Scotland, he was able to style himself 'King of all England, and of Denmark, of the Norwegians, and part of the Swedes'.

So Cnut was the first ruler of a united England and able to protect the country from attacks from Scandinavia, allowing trade and Christianity to flourish in a relatively peaceful atmosphere until his death in 1035. He has won the admiration of historians for his generosity, respect for justice and individual rights and the penance he did to atone for the sins of his Viking predecessors. One writer called him 'the most effective king in Anglo-Saxon history' – despite the fact that he wasn't Anglo-Saxon.

The exploratory expeditions of **Thorfinn Karlsefni** (980 – after 1007) are recounted in the Vinland sagas. He was the man who followed in Leif Erikson's footsteps in an attempt to found a settlement in North America.

Having settled in Greenland, Thorfinn and his wife Gudrid were persuaded by Erik the Red to voyage to the land discovered three years before by Erikson. They set sail in three ships, containing about 130 people, in around 1004 and settled in a region thought to be around the Gulf of St Lawrence shore. There, Thorfinn and Gudrid's son, Snorri, became the first European to be born on the North American mainland.

Encounters with local people, both friendly and violent, followed in the next three years before the colonists left their new homes and sailed back to Greenland.

Rollo of Normandy (c 846 – c 931) has been known by many names (Robert, Rolf, Rou, Hrolf, Rollon, Rollo the Walker or Ganger, Rollo the Viking) but one fact remains constant: he was the Viking who founded the French duchy of Normandy.

Rollo led raids on England, Scotland and Flanders before settling by the river Seine and taking part in attacks on Paris and Chartres around 911. The French king, Charles the Simple, was able to resist Rollo for a while but was eventually forced to negotiate the treaty of Saint-Clair-sur-Epte. This gave the Viking part of north-west France in return for a pledge of allegiance to the king, defence of the territory from Viking attacks and conversion to Christianity.

In time Rollo expanded his influence, his men began to marry local women and a capital of the new territory of Normandy – named after the Northmen or Normans – was established in Rouen.

Thought by many to be the finest skald (poet) of ancient Scandinavian times, **Egil Skallagrimsson** (c 910 – c 990) was also a fearsome warrior and, when he wasn't writing or fighting, a farmer. His story is told – and embroidered, no doubt – in Egil's Saga, thought to be the work of the author Snorri Sturluson.

Born in Iceland, Egil composed his first poem at the age of three, according to the saga. As a boy he exhibited berserk behaviour and when he was seven, having been cheated in a game, killed a playmate with an axe. Later he killed a retainer of Eric Bloodaxe and relative of Queen Gunnhild, and the latter two spent the rest of their lives trying to take vengeance.

Egil killed the queen's two brothers who had been sent to assassinate him and was declared an outlaw in Norway by Bloodaxe. Before escaping from Norway, he killed the king and queen's son and cursed them by setting a horse's head on a nithing (cursing) pole. For her part, Gunnhild cast a spell on Egil that is said to have made him feel restless and depressed.

When the rulers and Egil met again, it was in Northumbria, after the poet was shipwrecked. Persuaded by a friend that he should seek Bloodaxe's forgiveness, Egil composed a magnificent verse of praise that convinced the king that he should live.

Back on the farm in Iceland, Egil's last brutal act was the murder of a servant who had helped him to bury his silver treasure.

Olaf Tryggvason (c 964 – c 1000) was a Viking king who played a major role in the Christianisation of Norway.

Trained as a Viking warrior in Russia following the killing of his chieftain father, Olaf took part in attacks on England and in the invasion of the country with Sweyn Forkbeard in 994. He was confirmed as Christian in England the same year and returned to Norway to be crowned king on the death of Haakon the Great. Olaf set about imposing Christianity through force on the areas under his control, and introduced the faith to Shetland, Orkney, the Faroes, Iceland and Greenland.

He died in the Battle of Svolder, after which large areas of Norway reverted to foreign rule.

Saint Olaf was born Olaf Haraldsson in Norway in around 995, the son of a Viking lord. Becoming a warrior himself, he rapidly became known for his skills of leadership and strategy, and succeeded his father as head of a number of families who ruled parts of Norway.

During a trip to Normandy, Olaf was attracted to Christianity and was baptised at Rouen. He was inspired to return to his homeland to spread Christianity and unite the country, and he was recognised as king of a united Norway over a period of years. He was forced to flee to Russia in 1028 by an invasion by King Cnut of Denmark but, while in exile, had a vision that persuaded him to return to Norway so God could decide his fate.

Olaf set foot again in Norway in 1030, meeting Danish and rebel Norwegian forces at Stiklestad near Trondheim. His forces were outnumbered and the king fell to the blow of a rebel's axe. He was buried in a bank by the River Nid, from which a spring soon flowed that was accredited with healing powers. He was declared a saint in 1164.

Ingvar the Far-Travelled earned his fame for an attack against Persia between 1036 and 1042. There is plenty of discussion about who Ingvar actually was, but we know that he was a high-born man from Sweden who was worthy of his nickname.

It seems Ingvar travelled down the Volga river into what was known to the Vikings as Serkland in an attempt to reopen old trade routes. Some of his men took part in the Battle of Sasireti – part of a civil war in Georgia in 1042 – but the expedition was unsuccessful and, according to one source, only one of its ships returned home.

Harald Hardrada (c 1015 – 1066) was born Harald Sigurdsson, the half-brother of the Norwegian king who became Saint Olaf, and fought with him at the Battle of Stiklestad. After a period of exile in Kiev he returned to Norway in 1045 and became king two years later on the death of his nephew, Magnus Olafsson. He quickly won a reputation as a stern leader and earned the nickname Hardrada (hard ruler).

Having waged war against King Sweyn of Denmark, Harald laid claim to the English throne when Edward the Confessor died in 1066. His father's descendants had been promised the throne by King Hardicanute, he asserted. With Tostig, the brother of Harold of Wessex, he assembled around 300 ships and sailed to England, plundering and burning Scarborough and taking York. Harold Goodwin, told of Hardrada's intentions, answered: 'I will give him just six feet of English soil – or, since they say he is a tall man, I will give him seven feet.'

Harold's army arrived in Yorkshire on September 25, surprising Hardrada and Tostig at Stamford Bridge, near York. It is said to have been a hot day and the Norwegians had taken off their chainmail shirts, helping Harold and his forces to inflict terrible losses on them. Hardrada and Tostig were killed and fewer than 25 ships returned to Norway.

A descendant of Viking raiders including Rollo of Normandy, **William the Conqueror** (1028 – 1087) was an illegitimate child of Robert I, duke of Normandy. He was only eight when he himself became duke. Overcoming early difficulties in his dukedom – and known to his enemies as William the Bastard – he had conquered Brittany and Maine by 1064 and been promised succession to the English throne by Edward the Confessor.

But when Edward died in 1066 his brother-in-law, Harold Goodwin, claimed the throne for himself and William determined to invade England to stake his claim. With Harold delayed through having to defend his country against Norway in the north, William landed in Sussex with his army. Harold marched his weary men southwards and met the invaders in the Battle of Hastings on 14 October 1066. The death of Harold and his two brothers left the way clear for William, who was crowned king of England on Christmas Day.

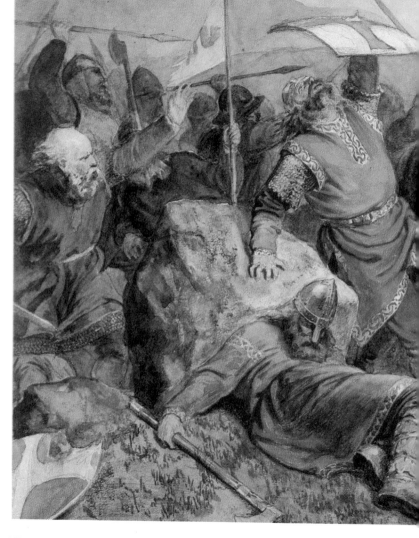

Right: *Death of St Olaf, by Peter Nicolai Arbo*

LITTLE BOOK OF **VIKINGS**

Legacy of the Norsemen

The murderous Viking assault on the abbey of Lindisfarne in 793AD undoubtedly came as a shock to the rest of England and other countries in Europe, and the ensuing events reverberate down the centuries. More than any other single event, it served to fix the image in the popular imagination of the Viking as a savage pagan intent on plunder and blood. And no matter how hard you try to dislodge the image from their minds, some people cannot be dissuaded from the notion that Vikings were nothing more than smelly, murderous brutes. The image is perpetuated to this day via the media of film, television and literature.

Mention the fact that Scandinavian peoples of the Viking Age excelled in art, were notable traders, diplomats, technologists and seamen, and pioneers in a kind of democracy, women's rights and civic society and you will probably receive some funny looks. But this, just as much as the horror of the brutal sacking of Lindisfarne, is the truth. It wasn't until the latter part of the 19th century that scholars outside Scandinavia began to re-examine Viking achievements and give credit where credit was due. The Vikings left indelible marks on history – marks that can still be seen today – yet still the myths persist.

One of the most visible reminders of the Viking presence in Britain lies very close to home: in the English language. Our ever-changing tongue was the beneficiary of Norse influence and remains so.

As we have seen, following the truce between King Alfred and the Viking warlord Guthrum in 878, England was

effectively divided into the Anglo-Saxon kingdom in the south and west and the Danelaw – very roughly what we know today as Yorkshire and the north-west, the east Midlands, parts of East Anglia and some of the Home Counties. The dividing line ran from London to Chester. It may be said that this was the original north-south divide, about which we hear much today.

Scandinavian settlement within the Danelaw – and the speaking of Old Norse – had an enormous impact in linguistic terms on Old English dialects. A melting pot of two languages was created by interaction between the settlers and their new English neighbours – interaction that included farming and trading together, intermarriage and eventual assimilation.

As time went on, the combination of the two languages spoken in the dialects of the north and the east Midlands made their way into the English spoken throughout the country. In fact, the east Midlands dialect later emerged as one of the most important contributors to the growth of the English we speak today.

One way of tracing the impact of the Viking tongue on English history is an examination of place names in the territories that once formed the Danelaw.

Telltale signs of Viking influence can be found in places whose names include the suffix –by, which meant homestead or village. Thus the east coast town of Grimsby can be seen to have once been Grim's homestead, while Derby was known as a village near deer. There are many examples, too, of place names ending with –thorpe, which meant 'new village' – Scunthorpe was originally Skuma's village. And the suffix -thwaite meant a meadow or simply a piece of land, giving rise to the meaning of Lothwaite – clearing on a hill.

Other place names indicate the intermingling of Scandinavians and Anglo-Saxons or the renaming of sites previously inhabited by the English. Most place names in England that begin with sk- show an Old Norse influence. The Leicestershire village of Skeffington, which means 'the dwelling of Sceaft's people', includes an old English element in the personal name Sceaft that was Scandinavianised, and a final element in –ton that meant 'farming village'. The further north in England you go, the more pronounced the Viking influence on place names becomes.

It should not be forgotten that Old Norse and Old English came from the same Germanic family and could be regarded as related dialects. That fact makes the identification of Old Norse elements in modern English quite tricky but far from impossible, and the results are often very satisfying. As we have seen with place names, words beginning with sk- often betray traces of the old Scandinavian tongue. So an everyday word like skin can be seen to be Old Norse in origin – it has descended from the later Old English scinn, which came from the Old Norse skinn. (Incidentally, the closeness of modern English to other Germanic languages can be gauged from the fact that skin is related to the Dutch and German schinden, meaning to flay or peel.) Another word we owe to Old Norse is sky: it comes from the word the Vikings used for cloud.

It's not only sk- words that betray Norse origins. Research the origins of common words like give, window (the old word meant, rather poetically, 'wind eye'), dream, get, take, egg, sister, husband, farming, happy, ill or muck and you will find the tongue of the Vikings lurking in the background. And another influence is to be found the areas of law and government – the word 'law' itself comes from a mixture of the Old Norse 'lagu' and the Old English diphthong æ. This demonstrates the importance of the legal system the Scandinavians set up in the Danelaw and the influence they had on law and systems of government.

Iceland's Althing is one of the world's oldest parliamentary institutions still in existence, dating from around the year 930. And it was brought into being by the Vikings who had colonised the island and brought with them their system of the settling of disputes and avoidance of disorder in society. The system revolved around the 'thing' – an assembly of the free men of a region, province or country. Western parliamentary democracy can be seen to be descended from the Viking 'thing', a system that also existed in other Germanic societies and was replicated in Anglo-Saxon England by the folkmoot.

The thing would meet at regular intervals to settle disputes, make political decisions and perhaps enact religious rites. This was where chieftains and kings were elected and where judgments were made according to the law, which was memorised and recited by the 'law speaker'. Presided over by the law speaker and the chieftain, a local thing would be represented at a higher-level thing responsible for a province or kingdom.

Right: *England in 878AD showing the extent of the Danelaw. Photo Hel-hama*

English territory

Danish or Norse territory

Celtic lands

swamp or alluvium

STRATHCLYDE

NORTHUMBERLAND

Bamburgh

Durham

IRISH SEA

York

NORTH SEA

THE DANELAW

Lichfield

DANISH MERCIA

Leicester

WALES

ENGLISH MERCIA

Cambridge

KINGDOM OF GUTHRUM

Chippenham

Wantage

London

Rochester

Edington

WESSEX AND ITS DEPENDENCIES

Canterbury

Winchester

Wareham

Exeter

ENGLISH CHANNEL

The theory of 'one man (or one freeman, at least), one vote' held sway at a thing, although in practice the more powerful members of society – chieftains and the heads of rich families – tended to dominate proceedings. But the power of the thing can be judged from an incident in the 11th century when a law speaker disillusioned King Olof Skötkonung of Sweden by insisting that it was the people, not the king, who held power. Realising that he was powerless against the thing, Olof gave way.

Today's 12-person jury is a remnant of the influence of the thing. Wrongdoers who were tried and found guilty at a thing faced one of three possible penalties: they could be fined or declared a semi-outlaw or a full outlaw. To be declared an outlaw was a harsh penalty indeed, for it meant that the guilty party was literally outside the law – he was banished from society and his property was confiscated. No one was permitted to help, feed or otherwise succour or support him. Perhaps worst of all – or perhaps not, given the terrible loneliness outlaws must have suffered – was the fact that anyone was allowed to kill an outlaw without fear of reprisal. No wonder outlaws often fled their country in search of comfort and normal society.

A thing could settle grievances by arbitration, with the parties in dispute agreeing on an objective third party to judge between them. If the dispute ended up at a thing, however, the loser could face a fine or being outlawed. Another, less subtle method of dispute settlement was the holmgang, a duel that was fought either to first blood or to death. While a thing had judiciary and legislative powers, it had no power to carry out a sentence – that was left to the injured party's family.

Things could last several days, and they were often enlivened by a festive atmosphere. Traders and merchants would try to make the most of the opportunity presented by these gatherings and brewers would help to create a relaxed ambience by providing barrels of ale and mead. There would often be hunting and fishing, the arrangement of marriages, the exchange of gossip and news and the renewal of old friendships.

The old Icelandic althing (literally all-thing) was held at Thingvellir, the 'assembly fields' located around 45 kilometres away from the site of the modern capital of Reykjavik. And it is interesting to note that the parliament of the Isle of Man, the Tynwald, is named after the place at which the island's thing met in times gone by, and that the word Tynwald is etymologically identical to Thingvellir.

Voting at the thing was strictly for free men; Viking women did not have a say in affairs of law or government. Women were under the authority of their husbands and could not act as judges, witnesses or chieftains. They could not go on Viking raids. In other respects, however, Viking women were more highly respected than their counterparts in other contemporary European societies. It would be a long time before European women gained rights denied them for centuries, but perhaps the Vikings were ahead of their time in this regard.

Viking women, for example, managed the family's finances and were responsible for the running of the farm when the husband was away on Viking business. When they were widowed, women were allowed to become rich and powerful landowners, and they were protected by law from unwanted attentions from men – there were penalties for offences ranging from kissing to intercourse. Evidence exists that one male transgressor of this law was fined two ounces of gold, a huge amount, as punishment for kissing a woman four

times. It was also considered shameful in Viking society to harm a woman, although violence against women during raids could and did happen.

An example of a woman gaining power on the death of her husband is told in one of the sagas. Aud the Deep-Minded had already been widowed when she left Norway for Scotland with her father and son. When the latter two were also killed, Aud determined to leave Scotland and, taking on the responsibilities of a man, secretly had a ship built and sailed for Iceland with her family and followers, stopping in Orkney to marry off a granddaughter. Upon landing in Iceland, Aud claimed land and settled, having arranged for a farm to be built. Once again she demonstrated her independence by running the farm and, as time went on, giving away parts of her land to supporters. Over the course of her life she attracted such respect that when she died she was afforded a funeral usually only granted to rich and powerful men – burial in a ship.

There is another area in which the Vikings left a very well defined mark that is still very much in evidence today – that of genetics. Studies have shown that, naturally, the genes of the Vikings are most often found in modern-day

Above: The Althing in Reykjavik, one of the world's oldest parliamentary institutions. Photo Dickelbers

Scandinavia: 35 per cent of males in Norway, Denmark and Sweden possess them, and that figure rises to 40 per cent in the west of Finland. However, examination of data from Britain and Ireland confirms that the Vikings were settlers as well as raiders.

A genetic and surname study in Liverpool, for example, showed a marked Norse heritage in up to 50 per cent of males, and there is a similar story in the Wirral and west Lancashire. These findings were similar to those in Orkney, which is known for the lasting impact of its Norse visitors and settlers.

So it seems the Vikings live among us still, and their impact took a far greater form than the destruction of some abbeys.

Find Out More

It is to be hoped that this little book will have provided the reader with plenty of useful – and mostly true – information about the people who came to be known as the Vikings. Or perhaps it has awakened a desire to learn more about peoples who have fascinated and thrilled ever since the first excursions from Scandinavia in the eighth century. If so, there is plenty of help at hand in the form of reading material and, if you wish to follow the Viking example and venture away from home, places to visit.

Books on the Vikings are easy to track down in public libraries and bookstores. For a glimpse – and a smell – of true Viking life, however, the UK-based reader should head for York and the Jorvik Viking Centre.

Jorvik is the term used by historians to describe the south of Northumbria during the late ninth and early 10th centuries, when it was dominated by Norse warrior-kings. The Jorvik Viking Centre, created by the York Archaeological Trust, uses the term to attract millions of visitors from all over the world, making it one of the UK's most popular tourist attractions.

Before the development of the Coppergate shopping centre got under way, the trust made sure the history of Viking York would be remembered for all time by conducting extensive excavations in the area between 1976 and 1981. What the archaeologists discovered was extraordinary: the well-preserved remains of some of the ancient city's timber buildings, along with workshops, fences, pens for animals, privies (toilets to you and me), pits and wells. There were also, of course, plenty of smaller artefacts from around 900AD among the haul of

more than 40,000 objects discovered: pottery, metalwork and bones were among them. The archaeologists were delighted to find that the wet clay of the area, due to its lack of oxygen, had even preserved materials such as leather, textiles and plant and animal remains.

The Jorvik, to use its popular, abbreviated name, recreated that part of the old city when it opened in 1984, greeting visitors with people, sounds and smells – the latter is always a talking

Above: *Coin making at York's Jorvik Centre*

point – from pigsties, a fish market and the aforementioned privies. As they travel round the centre in 'time capsules', visitors can hear people speaking in Old Norse, see inside their houses and back yards, be blasted by smoke from a blacksmith's furnace and whet the appetite with a whiff of stew cooking in the home of an amber worker. They can also inspect the remains of 1,000-year-old houses, artefacts taken from the excavations and Viking-Age timbers. Audio and video displays help to explain where the Vikings came from, why they ended up in York and how they lived and died – much as this book attempts to do.

The Jorvik's excellence in satisfying visitors' curiosity extends to explaining the types of weapons used in battle through the examination of wounds on skeletal remains, and shows how the Vikings continued to influence our world even after 1066 and the end of the Viking Age.

Among must-see museums for the Viking enthusiast is the Viking Ship Museum at Roskilde in Denmark, based near the scene of the excavation of five ships dating from around 1070 in the Roskilde fjord. This unique visitor attraction is in fact many things: a museum, a research institute and an active boatyard.

Basing its attraction on the five ships, the museum examines the Vikings' maritime culture, their shipping and shipbuilding, their craftsmanship and the voyages they undertook. The Ship Hall contains the five ships – two cargo vessels, two longships and a fishing vessel – while the story of the museum's historical and practical work with the ships is told outdoors in workshops. Reconstructed Viking ships are also on view.

This is not just a static display, though. The museum stages many water-borne activities throughout the year and younger visitors may be inclined to dress as a Viking. Other activities for youngsters include workshops in which they learn how to write their names with runes, while older visitors may be attracted by the offer of 'new Nordic Viking food' in the museum's restaurant.

Another Viking ship museum is to be found further north, at Bygdøy near Oslo in Norway. Part of the city's Museum of Cultural History, it is home to archaeological finds from Tune, Gokstad, Oseberg and a mound cemetery at Borre. Many fully or almost fully intact ships are on display but the stars of the show are the

Oseberg, Gokstad and Tune ships, and of these the fully complete Oseberg ship perhaps fascinates visitors most.

Discovered in 1904/05 in a large burial mound in Vestfold county, this ship was just part of a rich haul for the archaeologists. Also found were many grave goods – articles buried along with a body – and two female human skeletons. One of the women, whose burial dates from 834, was aged between 60 and 70 and suffered from arthritis. The other was between 50 and 55 years old. Archaeologists have been unable to determine which of the two women was more important – it's possible one was sacrificed so she could accompany the other in the afterlife – but it's clear that this was a very high status burial.

As for the Oseberg ship, it was found to be a clinker-built 'karv' vessel constructed almost entirely of oak. Visitors can see for themselves complex woodcarvings on the bow and stern, and can imagine the ship sailing at a speed of up to 10 knots on its coastal voyages. It is 21 metres long by five metres broad and fitted with a mast of about nine or 10 metres. Its 15 pairs of oar holes mean that it could be rowed by 30 people.

Visitors to Dublin will not want to miss Dublinia, a living history museum focusing on the Viking and medieval history of the city. It features historical re-enactment, with actors playing the roles of Vikings, and has recreations of houses and street scenes of the era.

These are just a few examples of the riches from history waiting to be discovered by Viking devotees. Good hunting.

Design & Artwork by Scott Giarnese

Published by Demand Media Limited

Publishers: Jason Fenwick & Jules Gammond

Written by Pat Morgan